3

38

62

from the staff

The invention of the rotary cutter revolutionized the quilting world. A round razor blade mounted on a handle and held flush against a straight edge makes cutting a line as simple as a wave of the hand. Along with ease and speed, rotary cutters reduce errors, making it easier to cut more squarely and more consistently. This accuracy makes finished blocks and quilts more precise. Thanks to this breakthrough in cutting, along with an abundance of beautiful fabrics and helpful tools, quilting has become an even more popular pastime.

Starting with basic strips and squares, and progressing to triangles, using templates, and the more advanced techniques of fussy cutting and squaring up blocks, this collection of timeless projects contains all the information you need to get started. You'll find the step-by-step instructions and easy-to-follow photos in the Rotary Cutting Primer invaluable resources for honing your skills. And we hope that the color options for many of the projects will inspire you to create your own unique color palette.

Whether you're an experienced quilter or just starting out, we hope this collection of quilts will bring you many hours of enjoyment.

happy quilting!

table of contents

D1402703

strips
& squares

Ready to get started with basic rotary cutting? Practice the fundamentals of rotary cutting with these simple quilting projects, each of which utilizes strips and squares in various formats. But even these basic shapes create dazzling designs with playful color placement and creative juxtaposition.

If you aspire to cut strips and squares proficiently, this quilt made with feed-sack fabrics in the perfect place to begin.

feed-sack
patches

Designer: Darlene Zimmerman
Photographer: Perry Struse

materials

48—6" squares of assorted feed-sack prints
1⅓ yards of solid green for sashing, border, and
     binding
1¼ yards of backing fabric
42×52" of quilt batting

FINISHED QUILT TOP: 37½×47½"

Quantities specified for 44/45"-wide, 100% cotton
fabrics. All measurements include a ¼" seam
allowance. Sew with right sides together unless
otherwise stated.

cut the fabrics

To make the best use of your fabrics, cut the
pieces in the order that follows.

from *each* of the 48 feed-sack squares, cut:
- 1—4" square
- 1—2×6" rectangle (you'll have 14 leftover
  rectangles)
- 2—2" squares (you'll have 27 leftover
  squares)

from solid green, cut:
- 5—2½×42" binding strips
- 4—2×42" strips for outer border
- 110—2×4" rectangles for sashing

assemble the quilt center

1. Referring to the Quilt Assembly Diagram,
below left, for placement, lay out the 48
feed-sack 4" squares, 63 of the feed-sack 2"
squares, and the solid green 2×4" sashing
rectangles in 17 horizontal rows.

2. Sew together the pieces in each row. Press
the seam allowances toward the solid green
sashing rectangles. Then join the rows to
make the quilt center. Press the seam
allowances toward the sashing rectangles. The
pieced quilt center should measure 32×42",
including the seam allowances.

add the borders

1. Sew together two assorted feed-sack 2×6"
rectangles to make a pair (see Diagram 1).
Press the seam allowance in one direction.
The pair should measure 3½×6", including
the seam allowances. Repeat to make a total
of 17 pairs.

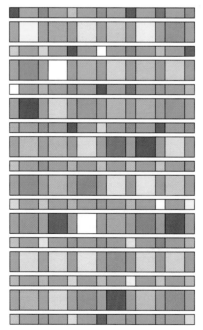

Quilt Assembly Diagram

Diagram 1

2. Referring to Diagram 2, cut each pair into
three 2"-wide segments for a total of 51
segments (you'll use 50 segments).

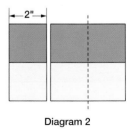

Diagram 2

3. Sew together 10 Step 2 segments and one
feed-sack 2" square to make the top inner
border unit. Press the seam allowances in one

direction. The top inner border unit should measure 2×32", including the seam allowances. Repeat to make the bottom inner border unit. Join the border units to the top and bottom edges of the pieced quilt center.

4. Sew together 15 Step 2 segments to make a side inner border unit. Repeat to make a second side inner border unit. Press the seam allowances in one direction. Trim the side inner border units to measure 2×45". Then join the border units to the side edges of the pieced quilt center.

5. Cut and piece the solid green 2×42" strips to make the following:
• 2—2×35" outer border strips
• 2—2×45" outer border strips

6. Sew the short solid green outer border strips to the top and bottom edges of the pieced quilt center. Press all seam allowances toward the outer border.

7. Add a feed-sack 2" square to each end of the solid green 2×45" outer border strips to make outer border units. Join the outer border units to the side edges of the pieced quilt center to complete the quilt top.

complete the quilt

1. Layer the quilt top, batting, and backing according to the instructions in Quilting Basics, which begins on page 94. Quilt as desired.

2. Use the solid green 2½×42" strips to bind the quilt according to the instructions in Quilting Basics.

hole in the wall

Designer: Julie Popa   Photographer: Perry Struse

Strips and squares cut from high-contrast prints create the illusion of a peephole in the center of each rectangular block in this quilt.

materials

3 yards total of assorted yellow prints for blocks
1½ yards total of assorted cream prints for blocks
2¾ yards total of assorted black prints for blocks and binding
½ yard total of assorted red prints for blocks
1½ yards of red stripe for border
7⅛ yards of backing fabric
85×99" of quilt batting

FINISHED QUILT TOP: 79×93"
FINISHED BLOCK: 10×12"

Quantities specified for 44/45"-wide, 100% cotton fabrics. All measurements include a ¼" seam allowance. Sew with right sides together unless otherwise stated.

cut and assemble block A

The cutting and assembly instructions that follow result in one block A. Repeat the instructions to make a total of 25 blocks.

from one yellow print, cut:
- 1—2½×4½" rectangle for position 1

from one cream print, cut:
- 2—2½×8½" rectangles for positions 4 and 5
- 2—2½" squares for positions 2 and 3

from one black print, cut:
- 2—2½×12½" rectangles for positions 8 and 9
- 2—2½×6½" rectangles for positions 6 and 7

1. Sew the cream print positions 2 and 3 squares to the short edges of the yellow print position 1 rectangle (see Diagram 1) to make the center unit. Press the seam allowances toward the cream print squares. The pieced center unit should measure 2½×8½", including the seam allowances.

Diagram 1

2. Referring to Diagram 2, add the cream print positions 4 and 5 rectangles to the long edges of the center unit. Press the seam allowances toward the cream print rectangles.

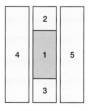

Diagram 2

3. Add the black print positions 6, 7, 8, and 9 rectangles in pairs according to the numerical sequence indicated on Diagram 3 to make a block A. Press all seam allowances toward the black print strips. Pieced block A should measure 10½×12½", including the seam allowances.

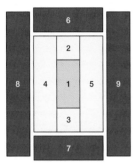

Diagram 3

cut and assemble block B

The cutting and assembly instructions that follow result in one block B. Repeat the instructions to make a total of 24 blocks.

from one red print, cut:
- 1—2½×4½" rectangle for position 1

from one yellow print, cut:
- 2—2½×4½" rectangles for positions 2 and 3
- 2—4½×12½" rectangles for positions 4 and 5

1. Sew the yellow print positions 2 and 3 rectangles to the short edges of the red print position 1 rectangle (see Diagram 4) to make

the center unit. Press the seam allowances toward the yellow print rectangles. The pieced center unit should measure 2½×12 ½", including the seam allowances.

Diagram 4

2. Referring to Diagram 5, add the yellow print positions 4 and 5 rectangles to the long edges of the pieced center unit to make a block B. Press the seam allowances toward the yellow print rectangles. Pieced block B should measure 10½×12½", including the seam allowances.

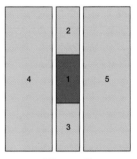

Diagram 5

assemble the quilt center

1. Referring to the Quilt Assembly Diagram, *left*, and the photograph *opposite*, lay out blocks A and B in seven horizontal rows, alternating the blocks. Sew together the blocks in each row. Press the seam allowances toward the A blocks.

2. Join the rows to make the quilt center. Press the seam allowances in one direction. The pieced quilt center should measure 70 ½×84½", including the seam allowances.

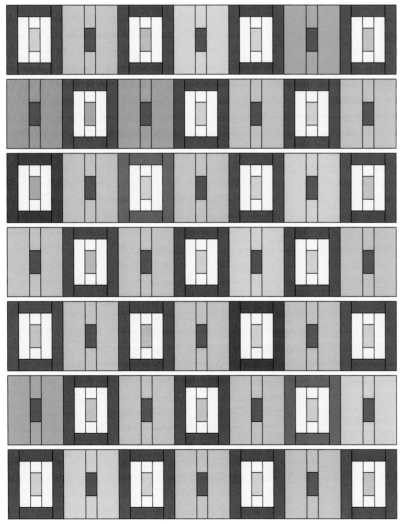

Quilt Assembly Diagram

cut and add the border strips
from red stripe, cut:
- 9—5×42" strips for border

1. Cut and piece the red stripe 5×42" strips to make the following:
- 2—5×96" border strips
- 2—5×82" border strips

2. Sew the border strips to the edges of the pieced quilt center, mitering the corners, to complete the quilt top. For instructions on mitering, see Quilting Basics, which begins on page 94.

complete the quilt
from one black print, cut:
- 9—2½×42" binding strips

1. Layer the quilt top, batting, and backing according to the instructions in Quilting Basics, which begins on page 94.

2. Quilt as desired. Quilter Paula Murray machine-quilted a variety of designs. She filled each block center with several rows of outline stitching and quilted circles in the cream print areas and border. She quilted horizontal loops in the black prints and a diagonal grid design in the yellow prints.

3. Use the black print 2½×42" strips to bind the quilt according to the instructions in Quilting Basics.

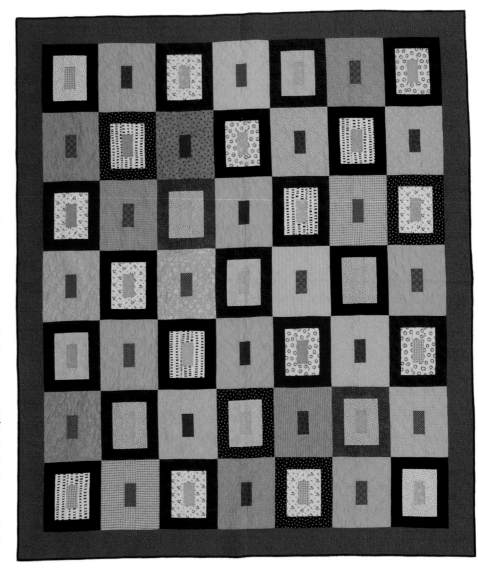

color options
a whole lot of fun
You can pare down Hole in the Wall to make kid-size quilts. These two color options use subdued pastels, *near right,* and eye-catching brights, *far right.*

On the pastel quilt, yellows, pinks, and blues of the same intensity were used for the A blocks, and the same pink and yellow prints were repeated for continuity on the B blocks.

For the brights version, the color placement was modified so the bright yellow is in the center of each block A, producing an even more pronounced keyhole effect.

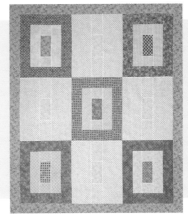
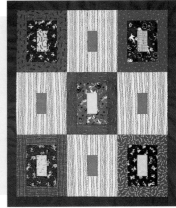

round the twist

Designer: Alex Anderson   Photographer: Craig Anderson

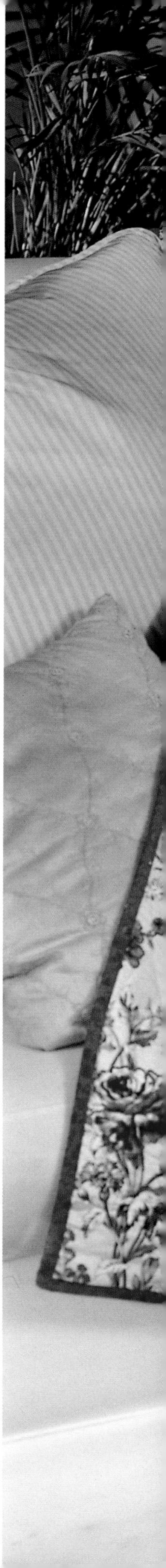

Careful color placement gives the illusion of interlocking blocks on this two-block quilt.

materials

1⅝ yards of solid cream for blocks
⅞ yard total of assorted green prints for blocks
1½ yards total of assorted pink prints for blocks and binding
⅓ yard of pink-and-green stripe for inner border
1⅔ yards of cream floral for outer border
3½ yards of backing fabric
62×74" of quilt batting

FINISHED QUILT TOP: 56×68"
FINISHED BLOCKS: 6" square

Quantities specified for 44/45"-wide, 100% cotton fabrics. All measurements include a ¼" seam allowance. Sew with right sides together unless otherwise stated.

cut the fabrics

To make the best use of your fabrics, cut the pieces in the order that follows.

The outer border strips are cut lengthwise (parallel to the selvage). The measurements given are mathematically correct. You may wish to cut your border strips longer than specified to allow for possible sewing differences.

from solid cream, cut:
- 32—6½" squares
- 31—3½" squares

from assorted green prints, cut:
- 62—2×5" rectangles
- 64—2" squares

from assorted pink prints, cut:
- 7—2½×42" binding strips
- 62—2×5" rectangles
- 64—2" squares

from pink-and-green stripe, cut:
- 5—1½×42" strips for inner border

from cream floral, cut:
- 4—6½×56½" outer border strips

assemble the snowball blocks

1. For accurate sewing lines, use a quilter's pencil to mark a diagonal line on the wrong side of all the assorted green and pink print 2" squares. (To prevent the fabric from stretching as you draw the lines, place 220-grit sandpaper under the squares.)

2. With right sides together, align two marked green print 2" squares with opposite corners of a solid cream 6½" square (see Diagram 1; note the placement of the marked diagonal lines). Stitch on the marked lines; trim away the excess fabric, leaving ¼" seam allowances. Press the attached triangles open. Repeat with two marked pink print 2" squares and the remaining corners of the solid cream 6½" square to make a Snowball block. The pieced Snowball block should still measure 6½" square, including the seam allowances.

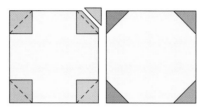

Diagram 1

3. Repeat Step 2 to make a total of 32 Snowball blocks.

assemble the twist blocks

1. Place a green print 2×5" rectangle along the top edge of a solid cream 3½" square. Sew together, stopping 1" from the top left corner (see Diagram 2). Press the seam allowance toward the green rectangle.

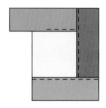

Diagram 2

2. Sew a pink print 2×5" rectangle to the right-hand edge of the Step 1 unit. Press the seam allowance toward the pink print rectangle. Then join a green print 2×5" rectangle to the bottom edge of the unit. Press the seam allowance toward the green print rectangle.

3. Add a pink print 2×5" rectangle to the left-hand edge of the Step 2 unit. Complete a twist block by sewing the remaining portion of the first green print rectangle in place (see Diagram 3). Press the seam allowances toward the rectangles. The pieced twist block should measure 6½" square, including the seam allowances.

4. Repeat steps 1 through 3 to make a total of 31 twist blocks.

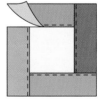

Diagram 3

assemble the quilt center

1. Referring to the photograph *opposite*, lay out the 32 Snowball blocks and the 31 twist blocks in nine horizontal rows. Designer Alex Anderson used a felt-covered design wall so she could easily rearrange the placement of her blocks at this stage. By doing so, she was able to achieve the appearance of the blocks interlocking with one another in several areas.

2. Sew together the blocks in each row. Press the seam allowances toward the twist blocks. Then join the rows to make the quilt center. Press the seam allowances in one direction. The pieced quilt center should measure 42½×54½", including the seam allowances.

add the borders

1. Cut and piece the pink-and-green stripe 1½×42" strips to make the following:
• 2—1½×54½" inner border strips
• 2—1½×44½" inner border strips

2. Sew the long inner border strips to the side edges of the pieced quilt center. Then add the short inner border strips to the top and bottom edges of the pieced quilt center. Press all seam allowances toward the inner border.

3. Sew a cream floral 6½×56½" outer border strip to each side edge of the pieced quilt center. Then add the remaining cream floral 6½×56½" outer border strips to the top and bottom edges of the pieced quilt center to complete the quilt top. Press all seam allowances toward the outer border.

complete the quilt

1. Layer the quilt top, batting, and backing according to the instructions in Quilting Basics, which begins on page 94.

2. Quilt as desired. Machine-quilter Paula Reid quilted flowers in the centers of the Snowball blocks and stitched a diagonal grid through the twist blocks.

3. Use the assorted pink print 2½×42" strips to bind the quilt according to the instructions in Quilting Basics.

color option
kaleidoscope of colors
Black fabric with variegated metallic flecks make the bright rings on this color option pop out against the dark background, creating a mesmerizing kaleidoscope look.

Fabric reminiscent of a watercolor painting makes a coordinating inner border to frame the quilt. If desired, the centers of the Snowball blocks are a great place to showcase intricate embroidery or quilting designs using variegated or metallic threads.

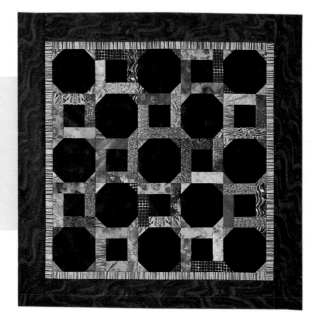

25 in 25

Take your quilting skills beyond the traditional Nine-Patch and make this quilt containing blocks of 25 squares.

Designer: Jill Abeloe Mead
Photographer: Perry Struse

materials

25—9×22" pieces (fat eighths) of assorted light to dark gray prints for blocks

6½ yards of white-on-white print for blocks, sashing, border, and binding

7¼ yards of backing fabric

86" square of quilt batting

FINISHED QUILT TOP: 80" square
FINISHED BLOCK: 10" square

Quantities specified for 44/45"-wide, 100% cotton fabrics. All measurements include a ¼" seam allowance. Sew with right sides together unless otherwise stated.

cut the fabrics

To make the best use of your fabrics, cut the pieces in the order that follows. The sashing and border strips are cut the length of the fabric (parallel to the selvage). The measurements are mathematically correct. You may wish to cut your sashing and border strips longer than specified to allow for possible sewing differences.

from *each* assorted gray print, cut:
- 5—2½×10" strips

from white-on-white print, cut:
- 2—5½×80½" border strips
- 6—5½×70½" sashing and border strips
- 9—2½×42" binding strips
- 20—5½×10½" sashing strips
- 125—2½×10" strips

assemble the 25-patch blocks

1. For each block you will need five matching gray print 2½×10" strips and five white-on-white print 2½×10" strips.

2. Referring to Diagram 1 for placement, sew together three matching gray print 2½×10" strips and two white-on-white print 2½×10" strips to make a strip set A. Press the seam allowances toward the gray print strips.

3. Cut the strip set into three 2½"-wide segments.

4. Referring to Diagram 2, sew together three white-on-white print 2½×10" strips and two matching gray print 2½×10" strips to make a strip set B. Press the seam allowances toward the gray print strips.

Diagram 2

5. Cut the strip set into two 2½"-wide segments.

6. Referring to Diagram 3, sew together the three strip set A segments and the two strip set B segments to make a 25-Patch block. Press the seam allowances toward the strip set A segments. The pieced 25-Patch block should measure 10½" square, including the seam allowances.

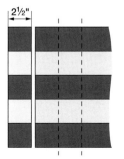

Diagram 1

Diagram 3

7. Repeat steps 1 through 6 to make a total of twenty-five 25-Patch blocks.

assemble the quilt center

1. Referring to the Quilt Assembly Diagram, *right*, lay out the twenty-five 25-Patch blocks, the twenty white-on-white print 5½×10½" sashing strips, and four white-on-white print 5½×70½" sashing strips in nine horizontal rows.

2. Sew together the pieces in the block rows. Press the seam allowances toward the sashing strips. Then join the rows to make the quilt center. Press the seam allowances toward the sashing. The pieced quilt center should measure 70½" square, including the seam allowances.

add the border

1. Sew the white-on-white print 5½×70½" border strips to opposite edges of the pieced quilt center. Press the seam allowances toward the border.

2. Sew the white-on-white print 5½×80½" border strips to the remaining edges of the pieced quilt center to complete the quilt top. Press the seam allowances toward the border.

complete the quilt

1. Layer the quilt top, batting, and backing according to the instructions in Quilting Basics, which begins on page 94.

2. Quilt as desired. Machine-quilter Sally Terry stitched a feathered medallion design in the center of each 25-Patch block and stippled in the four white patches nearest the center of each block. She repeated the feathered medallion design in the sashing and quilted a traditional feather design in the border.

3. Use the white-on-white print 2½×42" strips to bind the quilt according to the instructions in Quilting Basics.

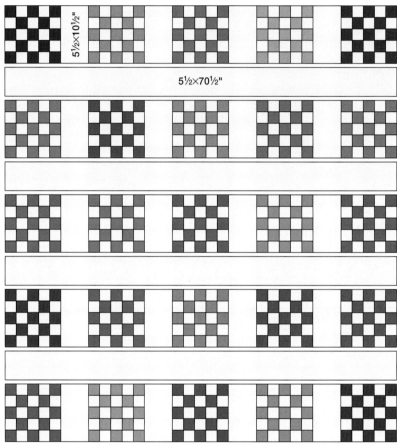

5½×10½"

5½×70½"

Quilt Assembly Diagram

color option
patriotic flair

If your tastes don't run to black and white, this quilt is equally striking when pieced in red, white, and blue. In this version, the sashing combines with an off-white print and blue check 5½" squares to set off the darker blue and red print blocks.

The wide border is also slightly different from the black-and-white version. It's pieced using a 3¾"-wide strip in the middle and 1¾"-wide strips on either side. A 6¼"-square cornerstone adds another dimension to the simple pattern. Or try using a single large print in the wide border and sashing to blend with colors in the blocks.

bow tie

Designer: Sharon Rexroad-Ericson
Photographer: Perry Struse

Rather than set in seams to make a traditional Bow Tie block, you can rotary-cut the fabrics and machine-piece the subunits to create this classic block with ease.

materials

1¼ yards of blue-and-white plaid flannel No. 1 for blocks

1 yard of blue-and-white plaid flannel No. 2 for blocks

1 yard of blue-and-black plaid flannel No. 1 for blocks

3½ yards of solid navy flannel for blocks

⅜ yard of solid medium blue flannel for inner border

2⅛ yards of blue-and-white plaid flannel No. 3 for outer border

1¼ yards of blue-and-black plaid flannel No. 2 for binding

5 yards of backing fabric

71×87" of quilt batting

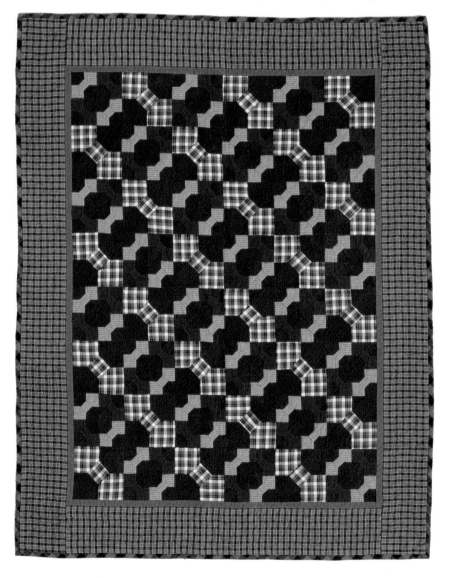

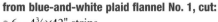

FINISHED QUILT TOP: 65×81"
FINISHED BLOCK: 8" square

Quantities specified for 44/45"-wide, 100% cotton flannels. All measurements include a ¼" seam allowance. Sew with right sides together unless otherwise stated.

cut the fabrics

Because flannel shrinks, designer Sharon Rexroad-Ericson recommends prewashing and drying all fabrics twice.

To make the best use of your fabrics, cut the pieces in the order that follows. The outer border strips are cut the length of the fabric (parallel to the selvage). The border strip measurements are mathematically correct. You may wish to cut yours longer.

from blue-and-white plaid flannel No. 1, cut:
- 6—4¾×42" strips
- 2—3×42" strips

from blue-and-white plaid flannel No. 2, cut:
- 7—2¾×42" strips
- 2—1¾×42" strips

from blue-and-black plaid flannel No. 1, cut:
- 7—2¾×42" strips
- 2—1¾×42" strips

from solid navy flannel, cut:
- 6—4¾×42" strips
- 14—2¾×42" strips
- 4—5½×42" strips
- 8—3¼×42" strips

from solid medium blue flannel, cut:
- 6—1½×42" strips for inner border

from blue-and-white plaid flannel No. 3, cut:
- 2—8×66½" outer border strips
- 2—8×65½" outer border strips

from blue-and-black plaid flannel No. 2, cut:
- 1—40" square, cutting it into enough 4½"-wide bias strips to total 310" in length for binding (For specific instructions, see Cutting Bias Strips below.)

cutting bias strips

Use a large acrylic triangle to square up the left edge of the 40" square. Make a cut at a 45° angle to the left

Bias Strip Diagram

edge (see Bias Strip Diagram). Measure 4½" from the cut edge and cut a strip parallel to the edge. Handle the edges carefully to avoid distorting the bias. Cut enough strips to total the length needed.

make the four-patch blocks

1. Align long raw edges of a blue-and-white plaid flannel No. 1 4¾×42" strip and a solid navy flannel 4¾×42" strip; sew together to make a strip set (see Diagram 1). Press the

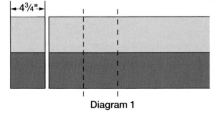

Diagram 1

seam allowance toward the blue-and-white plaid strip. Repeat for a total of six strip sets.

2. Cut the strip sets into forty-eight 4¾"-wide segments.

3. Referring to Diagram 2 for placement, sew together two 4¾"-wide segments to make a large Four-Patch block. To prepare the block for an upcoming step, clip the seam allowance just below the center intersection of the seams, cutting all the way to the stitching (see Diagram 3). Press the seam allowance as if it's in two sections, each one toward the plaid square (see Diagram 4). Repeat to make a total of 24 large Four-Patch blocks.

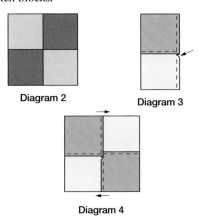

Diagram 2   Diagram 3

Diagram 4

4. In the same manner as for the large Four-Patch blocks, make a total of seven strip sets using blue-and-white plaid flannel No. 2 2¾×42" strips and solid navy flannel 2¾×42" strips. Cut the strip sets into ninety-six 2¾"-wide segments. Assemble the 2¾"-wide segments into 48 small Four-Patch blocks (see Diagram 5).

Using the blue-and-black plaid flannel No. 1 2¾×42" strips and the remaining solid navy flannel 2¾×42" strips, make 48 additional small Four-Patch blocks (see Diagram 5).

In the same manner as for the large Four-Patch blocks, clip and press the seam allowances on all of the small Four-Patch blocks.

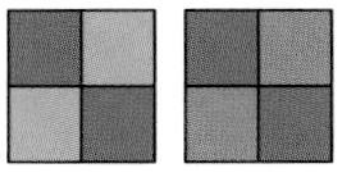

Diagram 5

cut the four-patch blocks

1. Place a large Four-Patch block on a cutting mat so the outer corners of the two solid navy flannel squares are on a single vertical line (see Diagram 6). This line on the mat will be referred to as the corner line.

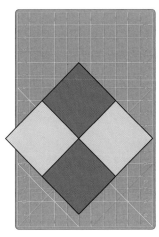

Diagram 6

2. Place your ruler over the block, aligning the 1" line on the ruler directly on the corner line (see Diagram 7). Cut along the edge of the ruler.

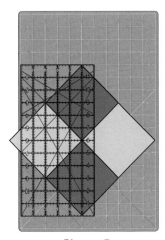

Diagram 7

3. Without moving the Four-Patch block, lift off the ruler, rotate the mat 180°, and set the ruler's 1" line directly on the corner line (see Diagram 8); cut. Discard the 2"-wide center section (see Diagram 9). Repeat with all the

large Four-Patch blocks to make 48 large triangles. The triangles do not need to remain in pairs.

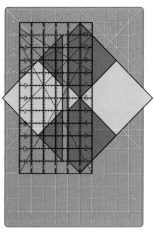

Diagram 8

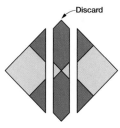

Diagram 9

4. Cut the small Four-Patch blocks into triangles in the same manner, except align the ruler's ⅜" line with the corner line. The section discarded will be ¾" wide. You will make 96 small triangles from each fabric combination for a total of 192 small triangles.

make the center units

1. Sew solid navy flannel 5½×42" strips to each long edge of a blue-and-white plaid flannel No. 1 3×42" strip to make a strip set (see Diagram 10). Press the seam allowance toward the plaid strip. Repeat to make a second strip set.

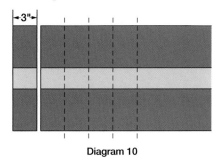

Diagram 10

2. Cut the strip sets into twenty-four 3"-wide segments for large center units.

3. Sew solid navy flannel 3¼×42" strips to each long edge of a blue-and-white plaid flannel No. 2 1¾×42" strip to make a strip set (see Diagram 11). Press the seam allowances toward the plaid strip. Repeat to make a second strip set.

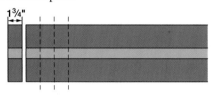

Diagram 11

4. Cut the strip sets into forty-eight 1¾"-wide segments for blue-and-white small center units.

5. Sew solid navy flannel 3¼×42" strips to each long edge of a blue-and-black plaid flannel No. 1 1¾×42" strip to make a strip set. Press the seam allowances toward the plaid strip. Repeat to make a second strip set.

6. Cut the strip sets into forty-eight 1¾"-wide segments for blue-and-black small center units.

make the bow tie blocks

1. For one large Bow Tie block you'll need two large triangles and one large center unit.

2. With raw edges aligned, center a large triangle over the center unit (see Diagram 12). There will be excess solid navy fabric at both ends. Sew the pieces together. Press the seam allowance toward the center unit.

Diagram 12

3. Repeat Step 2 with the remaining large triangle on the opposite side of the large center unit to make a pieced large Bow Tie block.

4. Center and trim the pieced block to measure 8½" square, including the seam allowances.

5. Repeat steps 1 through 4 for a total of 24 large Bow Tie blocks.

6. In the same manner, assemble 48 blue-and-white small Bow Tie blocks and 48 blue-and-black small Bow Tie blocks. Each pieced and trimmed small Bow Tie block should measure 4½" square, including seam allowances.

assemble the quilt top

1. Lay out two blue-and-white small Bow Tie blocks and two blue-and-black small Bow Tie blocks in two horizontal rows of two blocks each (see Diagram 13). Sew together the blocks in each row. Press the seam allowances toward the blue-and-white blocks. Join the rows to make a four-block unit. The pieced four-block unit should measure 8½" square, including the seam allowances.

Diagram 13

2. Repeat Step 1 with the remaining small Bow Tie blocks to make a total of 24 four-block units.

3. Referring to the photograph, on *page 18,* lay out the large Bow Tie blocks and the four-block units in eight horizontal rows, alternating blocks and units. Sew together the pieces in each row. Press the seam allowances toward the large Bow Tie blocks. Join the rows. Press the seam allowances in one direction. The pieced quilt center should measure 48½×64½", including seam allowances.

add the borders

The following measurements for inner border strips are mathematically correct.

Before cutting the border strips, measure your quilt center and adjust the lengths as necessary.

1. Cut and piece the solid medium blue flannel 1½×42" strips to make the following:
- 2—1½×48½" inner border strips
- 2—1½×66½" inner border strips

2. Sew the short inner border strips to the top and bottom edges of the pieced quilt center. Then add the long inner border strips to the remaining edges of the pieced quilt center. Press all seam allowances toward the inner border.

3. Sew the blue-and-white plaid flannel No. 3 8×65½" outer border strips to the top and bottom edges of the pieced quilt center. Then add the blue-and-white plaid No. 3 8×66½" outer border strips to the side edges of the pieced quilt center to complete the quilt top. Press all seam allowances toward the outer border.

complete the quilt

Layer the quilt top, batting, and backing according to the instructions in Quilting Basics, which begins on page 94. Quilt as desired. Use the blue-and-black plaid flannel No. 2 4½"-wide bias strips to bind the quilt according to the instructions in Quilting Basics.

triangles

Now that you've mastered right-angle cuts, you're ready to take your cutting one step further. Practice cutting squares in half and in quarters to make triangles that will give your quilting projects nearly limitless design possibilities. Triangles in all sizes give these quilting projects timeless appeal.

pinwheel panache

Designer: Meg Tryba   Photographer: Perry Struse

Triangles cut from multi-colored batik fabrics blend to create random pinwheels twirling across this quilt.

materials

1¾ yards of pink floral batik for blocks

4⅔ yards of pink print batik for blocks, outer border, and binding

1⅞ yards of purple floral batik for blocks and inner border

¾ yard of mottled dark pink batik for blocks

⅞ yard of mottled yellow batik for blocks

⅞ yard of mottled orange batik for blocks

¾ yard of mottled green batik for blocks

7¼ yards of backing fabric

86×98" of quilt batting

FINISHED QUILT TOP: 80×92"
FINISHED BLOCK: 6" square

Quantities specified for 44/45"-wide, 100% cotton fabrics. All measurements include a ¼" seam allowance. Sew with right sides together unless otherwise stated.

cut the fabrics

To make the best use of your fabrics, cut the pieces in the order that follows. Cut the outer border strips the length of the fabric (parallel to the selvage).

from pink floral, cut:
- 40—6⅞" squares, cutting each in half diagonally for a total of 80 extra-large triangles

from pink print, cut:
- 2—8½×92½" outer border strips
- 2—8½×64½" outer border strips
- 9—2½×42" binding strips
- 80—3⅞" squares, cutting each in half diagonally for a total of 160 small triangles

from purple floral, cut:
- 8—2½×42" strips for inner border
- 20—7¼" squares, cutting each diagonally twice in an X for a total of 80 large triangles

from mottled dark pink, cut:
- 5—7¼" squares, cutting each diagonally twice in an X for a total of 20 large triangles
- 16—3⅞" squares, cutting each in half diagonally for a total of 32 small triangles

from mottled yellow, cut:
- 5—7¼" squares, cutting each diagonally twice in an X for a total of 20 large triangles
- 24—3⅞" squares, cutting each in half diagonally for a total of 48 small triangles

from mottled orange, cut:
- 5—7¼" squares, cutting each diagonally twice in an X for a total of 20 large triangles
- 24—3⅞" squares, cutting each in half diagonally for a total of 48 small triangles

from mottled green, cut:
- 5—7¼" squares, cutting each diagonally twice in an X for a total of 20 large triangles
- 16—3⅞" squares, cutting each in half diagonally for a total of 32 small triangles

assemble the three-piece triangle blocks

1. Referring to Diagram 1, sew together a mottled dark pink large triangle and a purple floral large triangle to make a two-piece triangle unit. Press the seam allowance toward the purple floral triangle. Repeat to make a total of 20 pink two-piece triangle units.

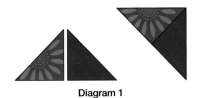

Diagram 1

2. Repeat Step 1 using the remaining purple floral large triangles and the 20 mottled yellow large triangles, the 20 mottled orange large triangles, and the 20 mottled green large triangles to make another 60 two-piece triangle units. Press all seam allowances toward the purple floral triangles.

3. Sew one pink floral extra-large triangle to one two-piece triangle unit to make a three-piece triangle block (see Diagram 2). Press the seam allowance toward the pink floral triangle. The three-piece triangle block should measure 6½" square, including the seam allowances. Repeat to make at total of 80 blocks, 20 of each color.

Diagram 2

assemble the pinwheel blocks

1. Sew together a pink print small triangle and a mottled orange small triangle to form an orange triangle-square (see Diagram 3). Press the seam allowance toward the pink print triangle. The pieced triangle-square should measure 3½" square, including the seam allowances. Repeat to make a total of 48 orange triangle-squares.

2. Sew together four orange triangle-squares in pairs (see Diagram 4). Press the seam allowances in opposite directions. Then join the pairs to make a Pinwheel block. The pieced Pinwheel block should measure 6½" square, including the seam allowances. Repeat to make a total of 12 orange Pinwheel blocks.

3. Repeat Step 1 using the remaining pink print small triangles and the 32 mottled dark pink small triangles, the 32 mottled green small triangles, and the 48 mottled yellow small triangles to make a total of 32 pink-and-dark pink triangle-squares, 32 pink-and-green triangle-squares, and 48 pink-and-yellow triangle-squares.

4. Repeat Step 2 to make eight dark pink Pinwheel blocks, eight green Pinwheel blocks, and 12 yellow Pinwheel blocks.

assemble the quilt center

1. Referring to the Quilt Assembly Diagram, *left,* arrange the 80 three-piece triangle blocks and the 40 Pinwheel blocks in 12 horizontal rows.

2. Sew together the blocks in each row. Press the seam allowances in one direction, alternating the direction with each row. Sew together the rows to make the quilt center. Press the seam allowances in one direction. The pieced quilt center should measure 60½×72½", including the seam allowances.

add the borders

1. Cut and piece the eight purple floral 2½×42" strips to make the following:
- 2—2½×76½" inner border strips
- 2—2½×60½" inner border strips

2. Sew the short purple floral inner border strips to the top and bottom edges of the pieced quilt center. Then add the long purple floral inner border strips to the side edges of the quilt center. Press all seam allowances toward the purple floral border.

3. Sew the pink print 8½×64½" outer border strips to the top and bottom edges of the pieced quilt center. Then add the pink print 8½×92½" outer border strips to the remaining edges of the quilt center to complete the quilt top. Press all seam allowances toward the outer border.

Diagram 3

Diagram 4

Quilt Assembly Diagram

complete the quilt

1. Layer the quilt top, batting, and backing according to the instructions in Quilting Basics, which begins on page 94.

2. Quilt as desired. Machine-quilter Rachel Tschumper quilted an allover design of swirls and curves in the quilt center and a rising sun design in the borders, all with variegated thread.

3. Use the pink print 2½×42" strips to bind the quilt according to the instructions in Quilting Basics.

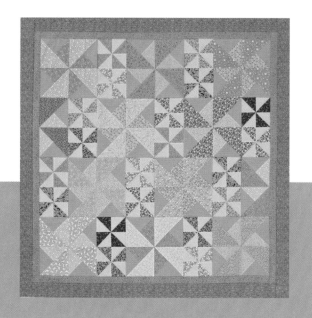

color option
1930s appeal

Pinwheels from another era spin on this more subdued color option.

The small-scale prints of the 1930s proved a perfect fit to the simple design of this two-block quilt. If you're unable to find vintage fabrics, don't worry. Many true-to-the-original reproduction fabrics are available at quilt shops.

Optional Size Chart for Pinwheel Panache			
ALTERNATE QUILT SIZES	**LAP**	**TWIN**	**KING**
Number of Blocks			
Three-piece triangle blocks	32	54	130
Pinwheel blocks	16	26	66
Number of Blocks Wide by Long	6×8	8×10	14×14
Finished Size	56×68"	68×80"	104" square
YARDAGE REQUIREMENTS			
Pink Floral	⅞ yard	1⅜ yards	2½ yards
Pink Print	3¼ yards	3⅞ yards	5⅔ yards
Purple Floral	1 yard	1½ yards	2½ yards
Mottled Dark Pink	½ yard	½ yard	1 yard
Mottled Yellow	⅝ yard	⅝ yard	1⅛ yards
Mottled Orange	⅝ yard	⅝ yard	1⅛ yards
Mottled Green	½ yard	½ yard	1 yard
Backing	3½ yards	4⅞ yards	9¼ yards
Batting	62×74"	74×86"	110" square

twist
and shout

Adept color placement in this bold lap-size quilt of triangle-squares allows for multiple design options.

Designer: Jane Huisingh   Photographer: Perry Struse

materials

⅝ yard of solid white for blocks and sashing
⅞ yard of purple batik for blocks and sashing
¼ yard of solid black for binding
36" square of backing fabric
36" square of quilt batting

FINISHED QUILT TOP: 30" square
FINISHED BLOCK: 12" square

Quantities specified for 44/45" wide, 100% cotton fabrics. All measurements include a ¼" seam allowance. Sew with right sides together unless otherwise stated.

cut the fabrics

To make the best use of your fabrics, cut the pieces in the order that follows.

from solid white, cut:

- 8—4⅞" squares, cutting each in half diagonally for a total of 16 large triangles
- 40—2⅞" squares, cutting each in half diagonally for a total of 80 small triangles
- 9—2½" squares

from purple batik, cut:

- 8—4⅞" squares, cutting each in half diagonally for a total of 16 large triangles
- 40—2⅞" squares, cutting each in half diagonally for a total of 80 small triangles
- 12—2½×12½" sashing strips

from solid black, cut:

- 3—2½×42" binding strips

assemble the blocks

1. Sew together one solid white large triangle and one purple batik large triangle to make a large triangle-square (see Diagram 1). Press the seam allowance toward the purple triangle. The pieced large triangle-square should measure 4½" square, including the seam allowances. Repeat to make a total of 16 large triangle-squares.

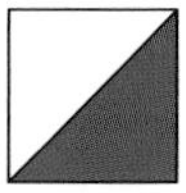

Diagram 1

2. Sew together one solid white small triangle and one purple batik small triangle to make a small triangle-square (see Diagram 2). Press the seam allowance toward the purple triangle. The pieced small triangle-square should measure 2½" square, including the seam allowances. Repeat to make a total of 80 small triangle-squares.

Diagram 2

3. Referring to Diagram 3 for color placement, sew together two small triangle-squares to make a pair. Press the seam allowance in one direction. Join the pair to one edge of a large triangle-square, again noting the color placement. Sew together three small triangle-squares to make a row. Add the row to the adjacent edge of the large triangle-square to complete the unit. Press the seam allowances toward the large triangle-square. The pieced unit should measure 6½" square, including the seam allowances. Repeat to make a total of 16 units.

Diagram 3

Optional Size Chart for Twist and Shout			
ALTERNATE QUILT SIZES	**TWIN**	**FULL/QUEEN**	**KING**
Number of Blocks	30	42	64
Number of Blocks Wide by Long	5×6	6×7	8×8
Finished Size	72×86"	86×100"	114" square
YARDAGE REQUIREMENTS			
Solid white	3⅝ yards	4¾ yards	7 yards
Purple batik	5¼ yards	7 yards	9¾ yards
Solid black	⅝ yard	¾ yard	⅞ yard
Backing	5⅛ yards	7⅔ yards	10 yards
Batting	78×92"	92×106"	120" square

4. Referring to Diagram 4 for placement, sew four units into pairs. Press the seam allowances in opposite directions. Then join the pairs to make a block. Press the seam allowance in one direction. The pieced block should measure 12½" square, including the seam allowances. Repeat to make a total of four blocks.

Diagram 4

assemble the quilt top

1. Referring to the photograph on *page 27* for placement, lay out the four blocks, the nine solid white 2½" squares, and the 12 purple batik 2½×12½" sashing strips in five horizontal rows.

2. Sew together the pieces in each row. Press the seam allowances toward the purple sashing strips. Join the rows to complete the quilt top. Press the seam allowances toward the purple sashing strips.

complete the quilt

1. Layer the quilt top, batting, and backing according to the instructions in Quilting Basics, which begins on page 94. Quilt as desired.

2. Use the solid black 2½×42" strips to bind the quilt according to the instructions in Quilting Basics.

color options
double the fun

Rather than piece the two-color quilt on *page 27,* you can have twice as much fun creating these two very different color options for "Twist and Shout."

For the first variation, *top right,* the same dark blue print appears in all four blocks, coupled with a pair of tone-on-tone pumpkin-hue prints. Placed block-to-block without sashing, some secondary patterns emerge from the quilt center. The sashing squares also are omitted on the outer border of this darker color option.

The second option, *below right,* is a whimsical multicolor quilt using 1930s prints. To emphasize the star motif in each block, muslin forms a consistent background along with a different print and solid. Muslin squares take the place of triangle-squares at the outer corners of each block. To unify the finished appearance of the quilt, two additional prints in complementary colors make up the sashing squares and strips.

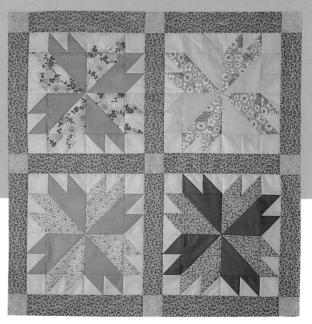

independence

Designer: Diane Hansen   Photographer: Perry Struse

Salute the red, white, and blue with a scrappy Triple Four-Patch design.

materials

¾ yard total of assorted gray prints for blocks and outer border

1⅜ yards total of assorted dark blue prints for blocks and outer border

⅔ yard total of assorted dark red prints for blocks and middle border

⅔ yard total of assorted black prints for blocks

⅔ yard total of assorted blue prints for blocks

½ yard total of assorted light gray prints for middle border

¾ yard of mottled blue print for inner border and binding

3½ yards of backing fabric

62" square of quilt batting

FINISHED QUILT TOP: 56" square
FINISHED BLOCK: 8" square

Quantities specified for 44/45"-wide, 100% cotton fabrics. All measurements include a ¼" seam allowance. Sew with right sides together unless otherwise stated.

cut the fabrics

To make the best use of your fabrics, cut the pieces in the order that follows.

from assorted gray prints, cut:
- 4—2½×22" strips
- 24—4⅞" squares, cutting each in half diagonally for a total of 48 medium triangles

from assorted dark blue prints, cut:
- 5—1½×42" strips
- 24—4⅞" squares, cutting each in half diagonally for a total of 48 medium triangles
- 4—2½×22" strips
- 48—2½" squares

from assorted dark red prints, cut:
- 5—1½×42" strips
- 44—2⅞" squares, cutting each in half diagonally for a total of 88 small triangles

from assorted black prints, cut:
- 2—9¼" squares, cutting each diagonally twice in an X for a total of 8 large triangles
- 6—8⅞" squares, cutting each in half diagonally for a total of 12 extra-large triangles

from assorted blue prints, cut:
- 2—9¼" squares, cutting each diagonally twice in an X for a total of 8 large triangles
- 6—8⅞" squares, cutting each in half diagonally for a total of 12 extra-large triangles

from assorted light gray prints, cut:
- 44—2⅞" squares, cutting each in half diagonally for a total of 88 small triangles

from mottled blue print, cut:
- 6—2½×42" binding strips
- 4—2½×40½" inner border strips

assemble the four-patch units

1. Aligning long edges, join a gray print 2½×22" strip and a dark blue print 2½×22" strip to make a strip set (see Diagram 1). Press the seam allowance toward the dark blue print strip. Repeat with the remaining gray and dark blue 2½×22" strips to make a total of four strip sets. Cut the strip sets into thirty-two 2½"-wide segments.

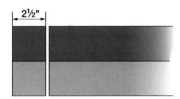

Diagram 1

2. Lay out two Step 1 segments as shown in Diagram 2. Sew together the segments to make a large Four-Patch unit. Press the seam allowance in either direction. The large Four-Patch unit should measure 4½" square, including the seam allowances.

Diagram 2

3. Repeat Step 2 to make a total of 16 large Four-Patch units.

assemble the double four-patch units

1. Aligning long edges, join a dark blue print 1½×42" strip and a dark red print 1½×42" strip to make a strip set (see Diagram 3). Press the seam allowance toward the dark blue print strip. Repeat with the remaining dark red and dark blue print 1½×42" strips to make a total of five strip sets. Cut the strip sets into 1½"-wide segments for a total of 112 segments.

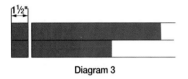

Diagram 3

2. Lay out two Step 1 segments as shown in Diagram 4. Sew together the segments to make a small Four-Patch unit. Press the seam allowances in either direction. The pieced small Four-Patch unit should measure 2½" square, including the seam allowances.

Diagram 4

3. Repeat Step 2 to make a total of 56 small Four-Patch units.

4. To make a Double Four-Patch unit, sew together two small Four-Patch units and two dark blue print 2½" squares in pairs (see Diagram 5, noting the placement of the red squares in the Four-Patch units). Press the seam allowances toward the dark blue print squares. Join the pairs to make a Double Four-Patch unit. Press the seam allowance in either direction. The pieced Double Four-Patch unit should measure 4½" square, including the seam allowances.

Diagram 5

5. Repeat Step 4 to make a total of 24 Double Four-Patch units. (You should have eight small Four-Patch units left over.)

assemble the triple four-patch blocks

1. Referring to Diagram 6 for placement, sew together two large Four-Patch units and two Double Four-Patch units in pairs. Press the seam allowances toward the large Four-Patch units.

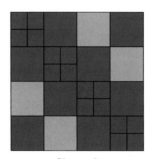

Diagram 6

2. Join the pairs to make a Triple Four-Patch block. Press the seam allowance in either direction. The pieced Triple Four-Patch block should measure 8½" square, including the seam allowances.

3. Repeat steps 1 and 2 to make a total of eight Triple Four-Patch blocks.

assemble the center block

1. Referring to Diagram 7 for placement, sew together four Double Four-Patch units in pairs. Press the seam allowances in opposite directions.

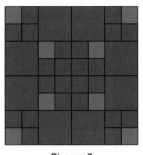

Diagram 7

2. Join the pairs to make the center block. Press the seam allowance in one direction. The pieced center block should measure 8½" square, including the seam allowances.

assemble the alternate blocks

1. Referring to Diagram 8 for placement, lay out one black print extra-large triangle, one black print large triangle, and one blue print large triangle.

Diagram 8

2. Sew together the two large triangles. Press the seam allowance toward the black print triangle. Then join the pair to the black print extra-large triangle to make an alternate block A. Press the seam allowance toward the black print extra-large triangle. The alternate block A should measure 8½" square, including the seam allowances.

3. Repeat steps 1 and 2 to make a total of four of alternate block A.

4. Referring to Diagram 9, repeat steps 1 and 2 using one blue print extra-large triangle, one blue print large triangle, and one black print large triangle to make an alternate block B. The alternate block B should measure 8½" square, including the seam allowances. Repeat to make a total of four of alternate block B.

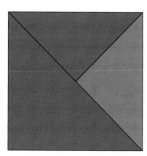

Diagram 9

assemble the triangle-squares

1. Join one black print extra-large triangle and one blue print extra-large triangle to make an extra-large triangle-square (see Diagram 10). Press the seam allowance toward the black triangle. The pieced extra-large triangle-square should measure 8½" square, including the seam allowances. Repeat to make a total of eight extra-large triangle-squares.

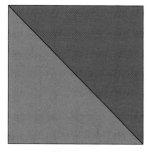

Diagram 10

assemble the quilt center

1. Referring to the Quilt Assembly Diagram for placement, lay out the center block, the eight Triple Four-Patch blocks, the four alternate block A, the four alternate block B, and the eight extra-large triangle-squares in five horizontal rows.

2. Sew together the pieces in each row. Press the seam allowances in one direction, alternating the direction with each row. Then join the rows to complete the quilt center. Press the seam allowances in one direction. The quilt center should measure 40½" square, including the seam allowances.

assemble and add the borders

1. Sew mottled blue print 2½×40½" inner border strips to opposite edges of the pieced quilt center. Press the seam allowances toward the inner border.

2. Sew a small Four-Patch unit to each end of the remaining mottled blue print 2½×40½" inner border strips to make two inner border units. Press the seam allowances toward the mottled blue print strips. Join the inner border units to the remaining edges of the pieced quilt center. Press the seam allowances toward the inner border.

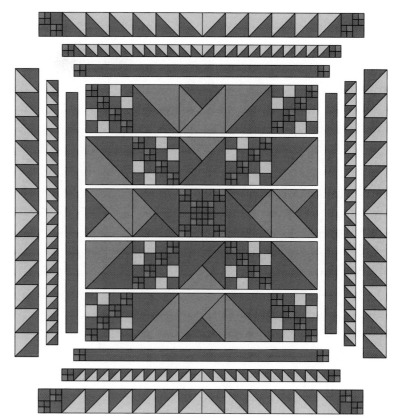

Quilt Assembly Diagram

3. Pair each dark red print small triangle with a light gray print small triangle; sew together to make 88 small triangle-squares. Press the seam allowances toward the dark red print triangles. The pieced small triangle-squares should measure 2½" square, including the seam allowances.

4. Referring to the Quilt Assembly Diagram on *page 33*, sew together 22 small triangle-squares to make a pieced middle border strip; note the direction of the red triangles. The pieced middle border strip should measure 2½×44½", including the seam allowances. Press the seam allowances in one direction. Repeat to make a total of four pieced middle border strips. Sew pieced middle border strips to opposite edges of the pieced quilt center. Press the seam allowances toward the mottled blue print inner border.

5. Sew a small Four-Patch unit to each end of the remaining pieced middle border strips to make two middle border units. Press the seam allowances toward the triangle-squares. Join the middle border units to the remaining edges of the pieced quilt center. Press the seam allowances toward the mottled blue print inner border.

6. Pair each dark blue print medium triangle with a gray print medium triangle; sew together to make 48 medium triangle-squares. Press the seam allowances toward the dark blue print triangles. The pieced medium triangle-squares should measure 4½" square, including the seam allowances.

7. Sew together 12 medium triangle-squares to make a pieced outer border strip; note the direction of the dark blue triangles. The pieced outer border strip should measure 4½×48½", including the seam allowances. Press the seam allowances in one direction. Repeat to make a total of four pieced outer border strips. Sew the pieced outer border strips to opposite edges of the pieced quilt center. Press the seam allowances toward the outer border.

8. Sew a Double Four-Patch unit to each end of the remaining pieced outer border strips to make two outer border units. Press the seam allowances toward the triangle-squares. Join the outer border units to the remaining edges of the pieced quilt center to complete the quilt top. Press the seam allowances toward the outer border.

complete the quilt

1. Layer the quilt top, batting, and backing according to the instructions in Quilting Basics, which begins on page 94. Quilt as desired.

2. Use the mottled blue print 2½×42" strips to bind the quilt according to the instructions in Quilting Basics.

color option
historical hues
Small-print fabrics in dark hues give this wall hanging a warm, rich look. The triangle-square borders echo those of the original; however, the mix of brown, burgundy, green, and blue give the light-colored diagonal squares in the quilt center added emphasis. The diagonal lines in this design would be even more obvious in a bed-size quilt.

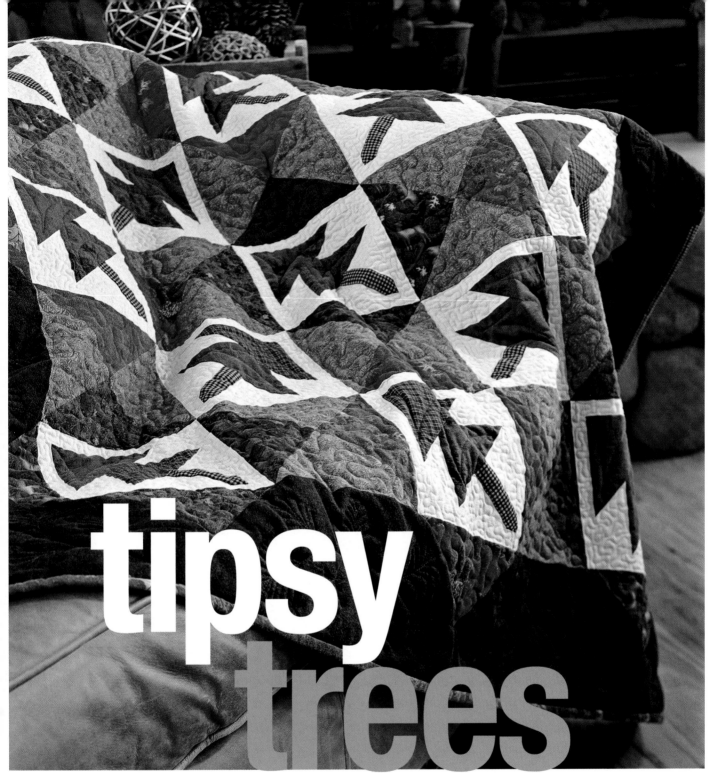

tipsy trees

Designer: Heather Mulder   Photographer: Perry Struse

Put this cozy flannel throw at the top of your gift list. After rotary-cutting the large pieces, you merely stitch and trim pieces to make the clever stylized pines.

materials

1¼ yards total of assorted green print flannels for blocks and binding

1¾ yards of solid cream flannel for blocks

⅓ yard of brown check flannel for blocks

1 yard of brown print flannel for blocks

1 yard total of assorted blue print flannels for blocks and binding

1 yard total of assorted red print flannels for blocks and binding

1½ yards of solid black flannel for blocks and outer border

3⅓ yards of backing fabric

59×75" of quilt batting

FINISHED QUILT TOP: 53×69"
FINISHED BLOCK: 8" square

cut the fabrics

To make the best use of your fabrics, cut the pieces in the order that follows.

from assorted green prints, cut:
- 18—5⅝" squares
- 18—5¼" squares

from solid cream, cut:
- 18—5⅜" squares, cutting each in half diagonally to make a total of 36 triangles
- 18—2¼×7" rectangles
- 18—2¼×5¼" rectangles
- 36—1¼×8½" rectangles
- 36—1¼×7" rectangles

from brown check, cut:
- 18—1½×9½" rectangles

from brown print, cut:
- 9—9¼" squares, cutting each diagonally twice in an X for a total of 36 triangles (you'll have 2 leftover triangles)

from assorted blue prints, cut:
- 5—9¼" squares, cutting each diagonally twice in an X for a total of 20 triangles (you'll have 3 leftover triangles)
- 7—4½×8½" rectangles

from assorted red prints, cut:
- 5—9¼" squares, cutting each diagonally twice in an X for a total of 20 triangles (you'll have 3 leftover triangles)
- 7—4½×8½" rectangles

from solid black, cut:
- 6—3×42" strips for outer border
- 10—4½×8½" rectangles for inner border
- 32—4½" squares

from remaining assorted green, blue, and red prints, cut:
- 20—2½×14" binding strips

assemble the tree blocks

1. Use a quilter's pencil to mark a diagonal line on the wrong side of the green print 5⅝" squares and the green print 5¼" squares. (To prevent the fabric from stretching as you draw the lines, place 220-grit sandpaper under the squares.)

2. Mark the center of the long edge on each of two solid cream triangles and the lengthwise center of a brown check 1½×9½" rectangle. Sew the marked solid cream triangles to each side of the brown check rectangle, matching the centers (see Diagram 1). Press the seam allowances toward the brown check rectangle. Trim the pieced unit to measure 5⅝" square, including seam allowances.

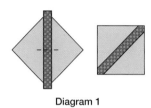

Diagram 1

3. Layer a marked green print 5⅝" square atop the pieced Step 2 unit (see Diagram 2; note the placement of the marked diagonal line). Stitch on the marked line; trim away the excess fabric, leaving a ¼" seam allowance. Press the attached triangle open. Trim to measure 5¼" square.

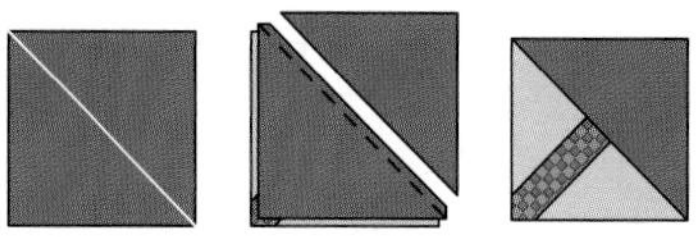

Diagram 2

4. Referring to Diagram 3, join a solid cream 2¼×5¼" rectangle to the top edge of the Step 3 unit. Then add a solid cream 2¼×7" rectangle to the right-hand edge of the unit. Press the seam allowances toward the cream rectangles.

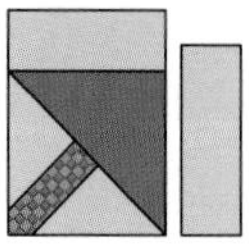

Diagram 3

5. Layer a marked green print 5¼" square atop the upper left corner of the Step 4 unit (see Diagram 4, *top right*; note the placement of the marked diagonal line). Stitch on the marked line; trim away the excess fabric, leaving a ¼" seam allowance. Press the attached triangle open.

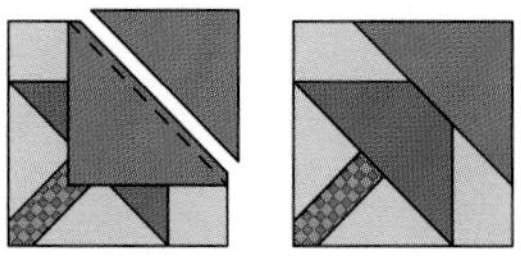

Diagram 4

6. Referring to Diagram 5, sew solid cream 1¼×7" rectangles to opposite edges of the pieced unit. Then sew solid cream 1¼×8½" rectangles to the remaining edges to make a tree block. Press all seam allowances toward the cream rectangles. The pieced tree block should measure 8½" square, including the seam allowances.

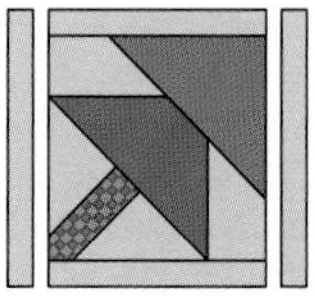

Diagram 5

7. Repeat steps 2 through 6 to make a total of 18 tree blocks.

assemble the hourglass blocks

1. Referring to Diagram 6, sew together a brown print triangle and a blue print triangle. Then sew together a brown print triangle and a red print triangle. Press the seam allowances in each triangle pair away from the brown print triangle.

Diagram 6

2. Join the triangle pairs to make an hourglass block (see Diagram 7, *opposite*). The pieced hourglass block should measure 8½" square, including the seam allowances.

3. Repeat steps 1 and 2 to make a total of 17 hourglass blocks.

Diagram 7

assemble the inner border blocks

1. Use a quilter's pencil to mark a diagonal line on the wrong side of 28 solid black 4½" squares.

2. Align a marked solid black square with one end of a red print 4½×8½" rectangle (see Diagram 8; note the placement of the marked diagonal line). Stitch on the marked line; cut away the excess fabric, leaving a ¼" seam allowance. Press the attached triangle open. In the same manner and again referring to Diagram 8, sew a second marked black square to the opposite end of the red print rectangle to make a red inner border block. Trim; press as before. The pieced inner border block should still measure 4½×8½", including the seam allowances. Repeat to make a total of seven red inner border blocks.

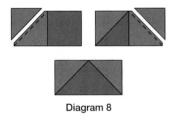

Diagram 8

3. Repeat Step 2 using the remaining marked solid black 4½" squares and the blue print 4½×8½" rectangles to make seven blue inner border blocks.

assemble the quilt center

1. Referring to the Quilt Assembly Diagram, *right,* lay out the tree blocks, hourglass blocks, inner border blocks, solid black 4½×8½" inner border rectangles, and four remaining solid black 4½" squares in nine horizontal rows.

2. Sew together the pieces in each row. Press the seam allowances in one direction,

alternating the direction with each row. Join the rows to make the quilt center. Press the seam allowances in one direction. The pieced quilt center should measure 48½×64½", including the seam allowances.

add the outer border

1. Cut and piece the solid black 3×42" strips to make the following:
- 2—3×64½" outer border strips
- 2—3×53½" outer border strips

2. Sew the long outer border strips to the side edges of the pieced quilt center. Then add the short outer border strips to the top and bottom edges of the pieced quilt center to

complete the quilt top. Press all the seam allowances toward the outer border.

complete the quilt

1. Layer the quilt top, batting, and backing according to the instructions in Quilting Basics, which begins on page 94.

2. Quilt as desired. Designer Heather Mulder machine-quilted a branch design in the borders and stipple-quilted in the hourglass blocks and around the tree motifs. She freehand-stitched designs in the trees.

3. Use the assorted print 2½×14" strips to bind the quilt according to the instructions in Quilting Basics.

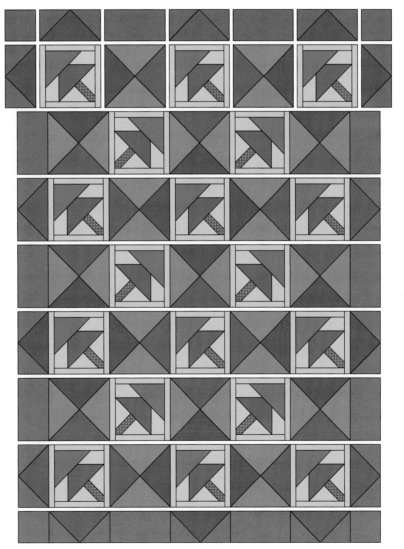

Quilt Assembly Diagram

building blocks

Designer: Peggy Kotek   Photographer: Perry Struse

The basic units of many projects—Flying Geese, windmills, and triangle-squares—have creative potential beyond classic quilts. Put a spin on these blocks by piecing them into pillows in bold, contrasting batiks.

pinwheel pillow

materials

2—6" squares of orange batik for block
2—6" squares of red batik for block
¾ yard of dark orange batik for border, binding, and pillow back
20" square of muslin for lining
20" square of quilt batting
14" pillow form

FINISHED PILLOW TOP: 14" square

Quantities specified for 44/45"-wide, 100% cotton fabrics. All measurements include a ¼" seam allowance. Sew with right sides together unless otherwise stated.

cut the fabrics

To make the best use of your fabrics, cut the pieces in the order that follows.

from orange batik, cut:
- 2—5⅞" squares

from red batik, cut:
- 2—5⅞" squares

from dark orange batik, cut:
- 2—14½×20" rectangles
- 2—2½×42" binding strips
- 2—2½×14½" border strips
- 2—2½×10½" border strips

assemble the pillow top

1. Referring to Diagram 1, use a quilter's pencil to mark a diagonal line on the wrong side of each orange batik 5⅞" square. (To prevent the fabric from stretching as you draw the lines, place 220-grit sandpaper under the squares.)

Diagram 1

2. Layer a marked orange batik square atop a red batik 5⅞" square. Sew the pair together with two seams, stitching ¼" on each side of the drawn line. Cut apart on the drawn line to create two triangle units (see Diagram 2). Press each triangle unit open to make two orange-and-red batik triangle-squares (see Diagram 3). Press the seam allowances toward the dark red batik triangles. Each triangle-square should measure 5½" square, including the seam allowances. Repeat to make a total of four triangle-squares.

Diagram 2   Diagram 3

3. Referring to the photograph, *above right*, lay out the four triangle-squares in pairs. Join each pair; press the seam allowances toward the dark red triangles. Join the pairs to make a Pinwheel block. Press the seam allowance in one direction. The Pinwheel block should measure 10½" square, including the seam allowances.

4. Sew the dark orange batik 2½×10½" border strips to opposite edges of the Pinwheel block. Sew the dark orange batik 2½×14½" border strips to the remaining edges of the block to complete the pillow top. Press all seam allowances toward the border. The pillow top should measure 14½" square, including the seam allowances.

complete the pillow

1. Layer the pillow top, batting, and muslin lining according to the instructions in Quilting Basics, which begins on page 94.

2. Quilt as desired. Designer Peggy Kotek machine-quilted a freehand design on the pillow top and stitched in the ditch inside the border. Trim the batting and lining edges even with the pillow top.

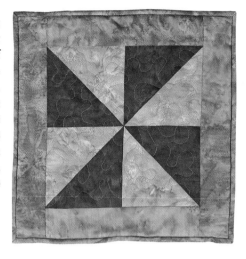

3. With wrong sides together, fold the two dark orange batik 14½×20" rectangles in half to form two double-thick 10×14½" pillow back pieces. Then overlap the folded edges by about 5½" (see Diagram 4) to make a pillow back that measures 14½" square. Stitch around the entire piece to create a single pillow back.

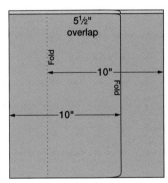

Diagram 4

4. With wrong sides together, layer the pillow top and pillow back; baste. Use the dark orange batik 2½×42" strips to bind the pillow cover according to the instructions in Quilting Basics. Insert the pillow form through the back opening.

windmill pillow

materials

¼ yard of lavender batik for block and corner squares

⅞ yard of purple batik for block, border, pillow back, and binding

22" square of muslin for lining

22" square of quilt batting

16" pillow form

FINISHED PILLOW TOP: 16" square

Quantities specified for 44/45"-wide, 100% cotton fabrics. All measurements include a ¼" seam allowance. Sew with right sides together unless otherwise stated.

cut the fabrics

To make the best use of your fabrics, cut the pieces in the order that follows.

from lavender batik, cut:

- 2—6⅞" squares, cutting each in half diagonally for a total of 4 large triangles
- 1—7¼" square, cutting it diagonally twice in an X for a total of 4 small triangles
- 4—2½" squares

from purple batik, cut:

- 2—16½×20" rectangles
- 1—7¼" square, cutting it diagonally twice in an X for a total of 4 small triangles
- 4—2½×12½" border strips
- 2—2½×42" binding strips

assemble the pillow top

1. Referring to Diagram 1, sew together one purple batik small triangle and one lavender batik small triangle to make a triangle unit. Press the seam allowance toward the purple

Diagram 1

Diagram 2

batik triangle. Sew the triangle unit to a lavender batik large triangle (see Diagram 2, *below left*) to make a Windmill unit. Press the seam allowance toward the large triangle. The Windmill unit should measure 6½" square, including the seam allowances. Repeat to make a total of four Windmill units.

2. Referring to the photograph at *left,* lay out the four Windmill units in pairs; join each pair. Press the seam allowances toward the purple triangles. Join the pairs to make a Windmill block. Press the seam allowance in one direction. The Windmill block should measure 12½" square, including the seam allowances.

3. Sew the purple batik 2½×12½" border strips to opposite edges of the Windmill block. Press the seam allowances toward the border strips. Sew a lavender batik 2½" square to each end of the remaining purple batik 2½×12½" border strips. Press the seam allowances toward the border strips. Sew the pieced border strips to the remaining edges of the Windmill block to complete the pillow top. Press the seam allowances toward the border. The pillow top should measure 16½" square, including the seam allowances.

complete the pillow

1. Layer the pillow top, batting, and muslin lining according to the instructions in Quilting Basics, which begins on page 94.

2. Quilt as desired. Designer Peggy Kotek machine-quilted the pillow top in a freehand design and stitched in the ditch around each triangle and corner square. Trim the batting and lining edges even with the pillow top.

3. With wrong sides together, fold the two purple batik 16½×20" rectangles in half to form two double-thick 10×16½" pillow back pieces. Overlap the folded edges by about 3½" to make a pillow back that measures 16½" square. Stitch around the entire piece to create a single pillow back.

4. Refer to Step 4 of Complete the Pillow on page 39 to complete the pillow, using the purple batik 2½×42" binding strips.

quilting tip

Carefully pressing seams is necessary for accurate piecing. Pressing is not the same as ironing. "Ironing" involves moving the iron while it has contact with the fabric; "pressing" means lifting the iron (with or without steam) off the surface of the fabric and putting it back down in another location. On the wrong side, press a stitched seam flat with the darker fabric on top to "set the seam." Then on the right side, position the tip of the iron on the lighter-color fabric. Glide the iron along the seam edge, moving from the lighter to the darker fabric.

flying geese pillow

materials

⅛ yard of lavender batik for blocks
¾ yard of indigo batik for blocks, border, pillow
    back, and binding
18" square of muslin for lining
18" square of quilt batting
12" pillow form

FINISHED PILLOW TOP: 12" square

Quantities specified for 44/45"-wide, 100% cotton fabrics. All measurements include a ¼" seam allowance. Sew with right sides together unless otherwise stated.

cut the fabrics

To make the best use of your fabrics, cut the pieces in the order that follows.

from lavender batik, cut:
* 16—2½" squares

from indigo batik, cut:
* 2—12½×18" rectangles
* 2—2½×42" binding strips
* 2—2½×12½" border strips
* 2—2½×8½" border strips
* 8—2½×4½" rectangles

assemble the pillow top

1. Use a quilter's pencil to mark a diagonal line on the wrong side of each lavender batik 2½" square. (To prevent the fabric from stretching as you draw the lines, place 220-grit sandpaper under the squares.)

2. Referring to the Flying Geese Diagram for placement, align a marked lavender batik square at one end of an indigo batik 2½×4½" rectangle; note the direction of the marked

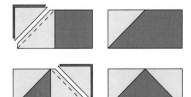

Flying Geese Diagram

line. Stitch on the marked line. Cut away the excess fabric, leaving a ¼" seam allowance. Press the attached triangle open.

In the same manner, sew a second marked lavender batik square to the opposite end of the indigo batik rectangle (again noting the direction of the marked diagonal line) to make a Flying Geese unit. The pieced Flying Geese unit should still measure 2½×4½", including the seam allowances. Repeat to make a total of eight Flying Geese units.

3. Aligning long edges, sew together two Flying Geese units to make a Flying Geese pair (see Diagram 1). Press the seam allowance toward the indigo batik triangle. Repeat to make four Flying Geese pairs.

Diagram 1

4. Referring to the photograph, *below,* lay out the four Flying Geese pairs in two rows. Sew together the pieces in each row. Press the seam allowances in opposite directions. Then

join the rows to make the pillow center. Press the seam allowance in one direction. The pillow center should measure 8½" square, including the seam allowances.

5. Sew the indigo batik 2½×8½" border strips to opposite edges of the pillow center. Sew the indigo batik 2½×12½" border strips to the remaining edges of the pillow center to complete the pillow top. Press all seam allowances toward the border. The pillow top should measure 12½" square, including the seam allowances.

complete the pillow

1. Layer the pillow top, batting, and lining according to the instructions in Quilting Basics, which begins on page 94.

2. Quilt as desired. Designer Peggy Kotek machine-stitched in the ditch around each triangle. Trim the batting and lining edges even with the pillow top.

3. With wrong sides together, fold the two indigo batik 12½×18" rectangles in half to form two double-thick 9×12½" pillow back pieces. Overlap the folded edges by about 5½" to make a pillow back that measures 12½" square. Stitch around the entire piece to create a single pillow back.

4. Refer to Step 4 of Complete the Pillow on page 39 to complete the pillow, using the indigo batik 2½×42" binding strips.

scrappy maple leaves

Designer: Jill Reber
Photographer: Perry Struse

Using scraps from your fabric stash, rotary-cut this simple project and capture the array of autumn colors in your yard.

materials

48—⅛-yard pieces of assorted red, gold, brown, and green prints for large and small Maple Leaf blocks, borders, and binding

¾ yard of tan print for large Maple Leaf blocks

1¾ yards of off-white print for small Maple Leaf blocks and sashing

5 yards of backing fabric

69×87" of quilt batting

FINISHED QUILT TOP: 63×81"
FINISHED BLOCKS: 6" square and 9" square

Quantities specified for 44/45"-wide, 100% cotton fabrics. All measurements include a ¼" seam allowance. Sew with right sides together unless otherwise stated.

cut and assemble the large maple leaf blocks

To make the best use of your fabrics, cut the pieces in the order that follows. These cutting instructions are for one large Maple Leaf block. Repeat the cutting and assembly instructions to make a total of 12 large Maple Leaf blocks.

from assorted red, gold, brown, and green prints, cut:

- 1—3½×6½" rectangle
- 1—3½" square
- 2—3⅞" squares, cutting each in half diagonally for a total of 4 triangles
- 1—1⅛×5¼" strip for stem

from tan print, cut:

- 1—3½" square
- 3—3⅞" squares, cutting each in half diagonally for a total of 6 triangles

1. Sew together a tan print triangle and an assorted print triangle to make a triangle-square (see Diagram 1). Press the seam allowance toward the assorted print triangle. The pieced triangle-square should measure 3½" square, including the seam allowances. Repeat to make a total of four triangle-squares.

Diagram 1

2. Aligning long edges, sew together the assorted print 1⅛×5¼" stem strip and one tan print triangle (see Diagram 2). Join a second tan print triangle to the opposite long edge of the stem strip to complete the stem unit. Press the seam allowances toward the stem strip. Trim the pieced stem unit to measure 3½" square, including the seam allowances.

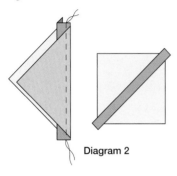

Diagram 2

3. Referring to Diagram 3 for placement, lay out the triangle-squares, stem unit, and remaining squares and rectangle in three horizontal rows. Sew together the pieces in each row. Press the seam allowances in each row in one direction, alternating the direction with each row. Then join the rows to make a large Maple Leaf block. Press the seam allowances in one direction. The pieced large Maple Leaf block should measure 9½" square, including the seam allowances.

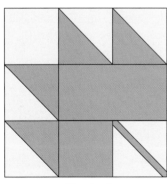

Diagram 3

cut and assemble the small maple leaf blocks

These cutting instructions are for one small Maple Leaf block. Repeat the cutting and assembly instructions to make a total of 36 small Maple Leaf blocks.

from assorted red, gold, brown, and green prints, cut:
- 1—2½×4½" rectangle
- 1—2½" square
- 2—2⅞" squares, cutting each in half diagonally for a total of 4 triangles
- 1—¾×4" strip for stem

from off-white print, cut:
- 1—2½" square
- 3—2⅞" squares, cutting each in half diagonally for a total of 6 triangles

1. Sew together an off-white print triangle and an assorted print triangle to make a triangle-square (see Diagram 1 on *page 43*); press. The pieced triangle-square should measure 2½" square, including the seam allowances. Repeat to make a total of four triangle-squares.

2. Aligning long edges, sew together the assorted print ¾×4" stem strip and one off-white print triangle (see Diagram 2); press. Join a second off-white print triangle to the opposite edge of the stem strip to complete the stem unit; press. Trim the pieced stem unit to measures 2½" square, including the seam allowances.

3. Referring to Diagram 3, lay out the triangle-squares, stem unit, and remaining squares and rectangle in three horizontal rows. Sew together the pieces in each row. Press the seam allowances in each row in one direction, alternating the direction with each row. Then join the rows to make a small Maple Leaf block. Press the seam allowances in one direction. The pieced small Maple Leaf block should measure 6½" square, including the seam allowances.

assemble the quilt top
from off-white print, cut:
- 30—1½×6½" sashing rectangles
- 7—1½×41½" sashing strips
- 2—1½×43½" sashing strips

1. Referring to the photograph *opposite*, lay out the small Maple Leaf blocks and off-white print sashing rectangles in six horizontal rows. Alternate the pieces in each row, beginning

and ending the rows with a block. Join the pieces in each row. Press the seam allowances toward the sashing rectangles.

2. Lay out the pieced rows and the off-white print 1½×41½" sashing strips; sew the pieces together. Press the seam allowances toward the sashing strips.

3. Sew an off-white print 1½×43½" sashing strip to each side edge to complete the quilt center. The pieced quilt center should measure 43½" square, including the seam allowances.

cut, assemble, and add the borders
from assorted red, gold, brown, and green prints, cut:
- 11—1½×20" strips
- 114—3½×6½" rectangles

from tan print, cut:
- 4—2×9½" sashing rectangles

1. Cut and piece the assorted print 1½×20" strips to make the following:
- 2—1½×43½" inner border strips
- 2—1½×45½" inner border strips

2. Sew the 1½×43½" inner border strips to the top and bottom edges of the pieced quilt center. Then add the 1½×45½" inner border strips to the side edges of the pieced quilt center. Press all seam allowances toward the off-white print sashing strips.

3. Aligning long raw edges, join 15 assorted print 3½×6½" rectangles to make the top middle border strip. The pieced top middle border strip should measure 45½×6½", including the seam allowances. Repeat to make the bottom middle border strip. Sew the top and bottom middle border strips to the top and bottom edges of the quilt center.

4. Aligning long raw edges, join 19 assorted print 3½×6½" rectangles to make a side middle border strip. The pieced side middle border strip should measure 6½×57½", including the seam allowances. Repeat to make a second side middle border strip. Sew the side middle border strips to the side edges of the quilt center.

5. Referring to the photograph, *below right,* sew six large Maple Leaf blocks in a horizontal row. Add a tan print 2×9½" sashing rectangle to each end. Press the seam allowances in one direction. The pieced Maple Leaf top border strip should measure 57½×9½", including the seam allowances. Repeat to make the pieced Maple Leaf bottom border strip. Sew the pieced Maple Leaf top and bottom border strips to the top and bottom edges of the pieced quilt center.

6. Aligning short raw edges, sew together 10 assorted print 3½×6½" rectangles to make the top outer border strip. The pieced top outer border strip should measure 3½×60½", including the seam allowances. Repeat to make the bottom outer border strip.

7. Aligning short raw edges, sew together 13 assorted print 3½×6½" rectangles to make a side outer border strip. The pieced side outer border strip should measure 3½×78½", including the seam allowances. Repeat to make a second side outer border strip.

8. Join the 3½×60½" top outer border strip to the top edge of the pieced quilt center, stopping a few inches from the outer edge (see Diagram 4). Sew a 3½×78½" side outer border strip to the left side edge of the quilt center, stopping a few inches from the outer edge. Finish sewing the top outer border strip to the quilt center.

9. Sew the 3½×60½" bottom outer border strip to the bottom edge of the pieced quilt center, stopping a few inches from the outer edge. Finish sewing the left side outer border strip to the quilt center. Sew the remaining 3½×78½" outer border strip to the right side edge of the quilt center. Finish sewing the bottom outer border strip to the quilt center to complete the quilt. Press the seam allowances toward the outer border.

complete the quilt

from assorted red, gold, brown, and green prints, cut:

- 16—2½×20" binding strips

Layer the quilt top, batting, and backing according to the instructions in Quilting Basics, which begins on page 94. Quilt as desired. Use the assorted print 2½×20" strips to bind the quilt according to the instructions in Quilting Basics.

color option
turn over a new leaf
Bright hues, rather than the muted browns and golds of autumn, assure this cheerful wall hanging a prominent place in your decorating scheme any time of year.

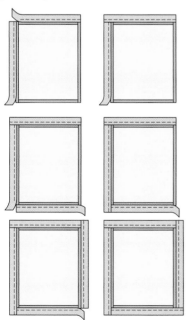

Diagram 4

Make a bold statement with batik
Flying Geese blocks set in vertical rows.

heading north

Designer: Mabeth Oxenreider
Photographer: Marcia Cameron

materials

2½ yards total of assorted batiks for blocks
2 yards of bright blue print for sashing, border, and binding
54×66" of quilt batting
3 yards of backing fabric

FINISHED QUILT TOP: 48×60"
FINISHED BLOCK: 3×6"

Quantities specified for 44/45"-wide, 100% cotton fabrics. All measurements include a ¼" seam allowance. Sew with right sides together unless otherwise stated.

cut the fabrics

To make the best use of your fabrics, cut the pieces in the order that follows.

The sashing and border strips are cut lengthwise (parallel to the selvage). The measurements given are mathematically correct. You may wish to cut your strips longer than specified to allow for possible sewing differences.

from assorted batiks, cut:
- 64—3½×6½" rectangles
- 128—3½" squares

from bright blue print, cut:
- 4—6½×48½" border strips
- 3—4½×48½" sashing strips
- 6—2½×42" binding strips

assemble the blocks

1. For accurate sewing lines, use a quilter's pencil to mark a diagonal line on the wrong side of each batik 3½" square. (To prevent your fabric from stretching as you draw the lines, place 220-grit sandpaper under the squares.)

2. Referring to the Flying Geese Diagram, align a marked batik square with one end of a batik 3½×6½" rectangle; note the placement of the marked line. Stitch on the marked line. Cut away the excess fabric, leaving a ¼" seam allowance. Press the attached triangle open. In the same manner, sew a second marked batik square to the opposite end of the batik rectangle to make a Flying Geese block. The pieced Flying Geese block should still measure 3½×6½", including the seam allowances. Repeat to make a total of 64 Flying Geese blocks.

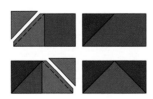

Flying Geese Diagram

assemble the quilt center

1. Referring to the photograph, *opposite*, for placement, lay out the Flying Geese blocks in four vertical rows of 16 each. Sew together the blocks in each row. Press the seam allowances in one direction. Each pieced Flying Geese row should measure 6½×48½", including the seam allowances.

2. Sew together the three bright blue print 4½×48½" sashing strips and the four Flying Geese rows to make the quilt center. Press the seam allowances toward the sashing strips. The pieced quilt center should measure 36½×48½", including the seam allowances.

add the border

1. Sew a bright blue print 6½×48½" border strip to each side edge of the pieced quilt center. Press the seam allowances toward the border.

2. Sew the remaining bright blue print 6½×48½" border strips to the top and bottom edges of the pieced quilt center to complete the quilt top.

complete the quilt

1. Layer the quilt top, batting, and backing according to the instructions in Quilting Basics, page 94. Quilt as desired.

2. Use the bright blue print 2½×42" strips to bind the quilt according to the instructions in Quilting Basics.

using templates

Even though the invention of the rotary cutter has freed quilters from the rigors of tedious measuring and cutting, templates are often an easier way to cut irregular shapes. Use your rotary cutter in combination with plastic templates to make quick work of cutting shapes that require a pattern.

streaks of lightning

Designers: Jill Reber and Lynn Johnson   Photographer: Perry Struse

Even though it's possible to rotary-cut 60° triangles, it's easier and speedier when you rotary-cut them using a template. Use our pattern to create your own template, then rotary-cut the triangles before piecing them together in a zigzag fashion.

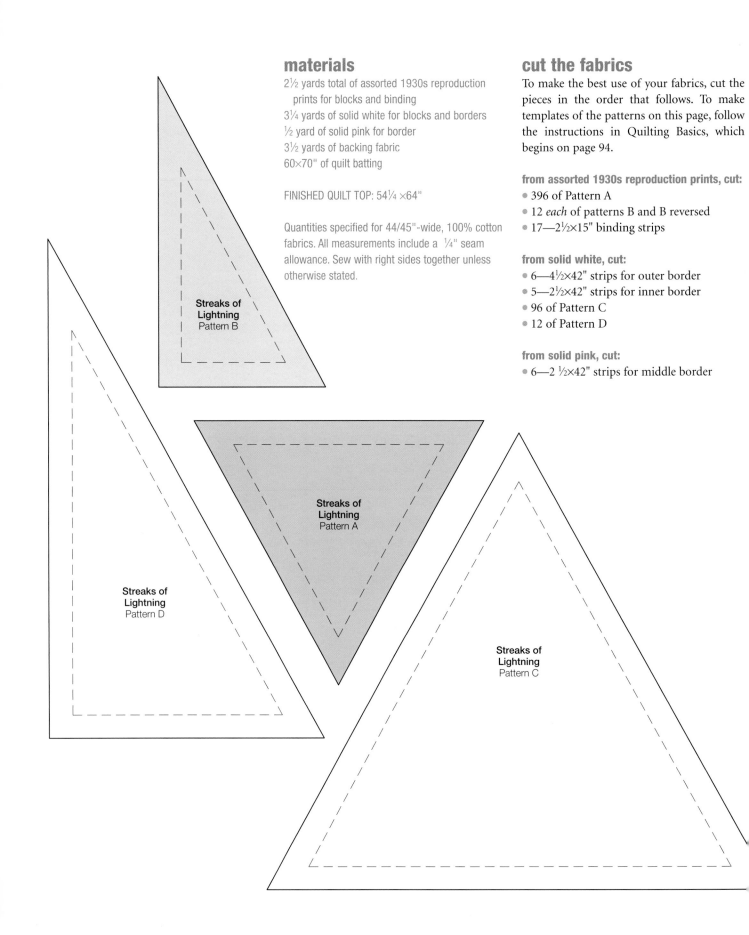

materials

2½ yards total of assorted 1930s reproduction prints for blocks and binding

3¼ yards of solid white for blocks and borders

½ yard of solid pink for border

3½ yards of backing fabric

60×70" of quilt batting

FINISHED QUILT TOP: 54¼ ×64"

Quantities specified for 44/45"-wide, 100% cotton fabrics. All measurements include a ¼" seam allowance. Sew with right sides together unless otherwise stated.

cut the fabrics

To make the best use of your fabrics, cut the pieces in the order that follows. To make templates of the patterns on this page, follow the instructions in Quilting Basics, which begins on page 94.

from assorted 1930s reproduction prints, cut:
- 396 of Pattern A
- 12 *each* of patterns B and B reversed
- 17—2½×15" binding strips

from solid white, cut:
- 6—4½×42" strips for outer border
- 5—2½×42" strips for inner border
- 96 of Pattern C
- 12 of Pattern D

from solid pink, cut:
- 6—2 ½×42" strips for middle border

Streaks of Lightning
Pattern B

Streaks of Lightning
Pattern A

Streaks of Lightning
Pattern D

Streaks of Lightning
Pattern C

assemble the blocks

1. Referring to Diagram 1, sew together three assorted print A triangles. Press the seam allowances toward the outside triangles. Add a fourth assorted print A triangle to the top edge of the subunit to make a Unit A. Press the seam allowance toward the top triangle. Repeat for a total of 96 of Unit A.

Diagram 1

2. Referring to Diagram 2, join an assorted print A triangle, an assorted print B reversed triangle, and an assorted print B triangle to make a Unit B. Press the seam allowances toward the A and B triangles. Repeat for a total of 12 of Unit B.

Diagram 2

assemble the quilt center

1. Referring to Diagram 3 for placement, lay out eight of Unit A, one of Unit B, eight solid white C triangles, and one solid white D triangle in a horizontal row. Sew together the triangles in the row. Press the seam allowances toward the solid white triangles. The pieced row should measure 38³⁄₄×4¹⁄₂", including the seam allowances.

Diagram 3

2. Repeat Step 1 to make a total of 12 rows.

3. Referring to the photograph on *page 49*, lay out the rows, reversing every other row. (Note how designer Lynn Johnson reversed every other row.) Then join the rows. Press the seam allowances in one direction. The pieced quilt center should measure 38³⁄₄×48¹⁄₂", including the seam allowances.

add the borders

1. Cut and piece the solid white 2¹⁄₂×42" strips to make the following:
- 2—2¹⁄₂×38³⁄₄" inner border strips
- 2—2¹⁄₂×52¹⁄₂" inner border strips

2. Sew one solid white 2¹⁄₂×38³⁄₄" border strip to the top edge and one to the bottom edge of the pieced quilt center. Then add a solid white 2¹⁄₂×52¹⁄₂" border strip to each side edge of the pieced quilt center. Press the seam allowances toward the solid white border.

3. Cut and piece the solid pink 2¹⁄₂×42" strips to make the following:
- 2—2¹⁄₂×42³⁄₄" middle border strips
- 2—2¹⁄₂×56¹⁄₂" middle border strips

4. Sew one solid pink 2¹⁄₂×42³⁄₄" border strip to the top edge and one to the bottom edge of the pieced quilt center. Then add a solid pink 2¹⁄₂×56¹⁄₂" border strip to each side edge of the pieced quilt center. Press the seam allowances toward the solid pink border.

5. Cut and piece the solid white 4¹⁄₂×42" strips to make the following:
- 2—4¹⁄₂×46³⁄₄" outer border strips
- 2—4¹⁄₂×64¹⁄₂" outer border strips

6. Sew one solid white 4¹⁄₂×46³⁄₄" border strip to the top edge and one to the bottom edge of the pieced quilt center. Then add a solid white 4¹⁄₂×64¹⁄₂" border strip to each side edge of the pieced quilt center. Press the seam allowances toward the solid white border.

complete the quilt

Layer the quilt top, batting, and backing according to the instructions in Quilting Basics, which begins on page 94. Quilt as desired. Use the assorted print 2¹⁄₂×15" strips to bind the quilt according to the instructions in Quilting Basics.

color option
zigzag delight

An assortment of red, blue, and cream prints and plaids was used for this variation of Streaks of Lightning. Alternating rows of either red or blue create a strong contrast with the cream in between.

snow stars

Designer: Joy Hoffman   Photographer: Perry Struse

Cool winter colors of blue and white give this bed-size quilt a clean, crisp finish. Whether you choose this color combination or a more dramatic grouping, you're sure to find this project of Four-Patch blocks and triangle units easy to piece.

materials

2½ yards of dark blue print for blocks, border, and binding
3¾ yards of light blue print for blocks and border
2⅜ yards of white print for blocks and border
4½ yards of backing fabric
79×94" of quilt batting

FINISHED QUILT TOP: 72½×87½"
FINISHED BLOCK: 12½" square

Quantities specified for 44/45"-wide, 100% cotton fabrics. All measurements include a ¼" seam allowance unless otherwise stated.

cut the fabrics

To make the best use of your fabrics, cut the pieces in the order that follows.

from dark blue print, cut:
- 8—2½×42" binding strips
- 14—1¾×42" strips for Four-Patch units
- 12—3" sashing squares
- 36—3×1¾" E rectangles
- 36—3×4¼" F rectangles
- 18—3×6¾" G rectangles
- 14—3×5½" H rectangles
- 28—3" C squares

from light blue print, cut:
- 80 Snow Stars Triangle Pattern
- 31—3×13" sashing strips
- 7—1¾×42" strips for Four-Patch units
- 8—3×8" A rectangles
- 4—3×5½" B rectangles
- 188—3" C squares
- 14—1¾×3" D rectangles

from white print, cut:
- 28—1¾×42" strips for border and Four-Patch units
- 80 Snow Stars Triangle Pattern

assemble the block units
four-patch units

1. Aligning long raw edges, sew together one dark blue print 1¾×42" strip and one white print 1¾×42" strip to make a strip set. Press the seam allowance toward the dark blue strip. Repeat to make a total of 14 strip sets.

2. Referring to Diagram 1, cut a 1¾"-wide segment from a strip set. Repeat for a total of 320 segments.

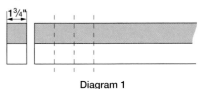

Diagram 1

3. Sew together two 1¾"-wide segments from Step 2 to make a small Four-Patch unit (see Diagram 2). Press the seam allowance in one direction. The pieced small Four-Patch unit should measure 3" square, including the seam allowances. Repeat to make a total of 160 small Four-Patch units.

Diagram 2

4. To make a large Four-Patch unit you'll need two small Four-Patch units and two light blue print C squares.

5. Referring to Diagram 3 for placement, lay out the Four-Patch units and squares in two rows. Sew together the squares in each row. Press the seam allowances toward the light blue print squares. Join the rows. Press the seam allowance in one direction. The pieced large Four-Patch unit should measure 5½" square, including the seam allowances. Repeat to make a total of 80 large Four-Patch units.

Diagram 3

triangle units

Referring to Diagram 4, join one white print triangle and one light blue print triangle. Press the seam allowance toward the light blue triangle. The pieced triangle unit should measure 3×5½", including the seam allowances. Repeat to make a total of 80 triangle units.

Diagram 4

assemble the blocks

1. For one block you'll need four large Four-Patch units, four triangle units, and one light blue C square.

2. Referring to Diagram 5 for placement, lay out the units and square in three horizontal rows. Sew together the pieces in each row. Press the seam allowances toward the triangle units. Then join the rows. The pieced block should measure 13" square, including the seam allowances.

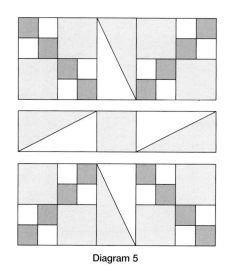

Diagram 5

3. Repeat steps 1 and 2 to make a total of 20 blocks.

assemble the quilt top

Referring to the photograph, *opposite*, for placement, lay out the blocks, sashing strips, and sashing squares in horizontal rows. Sew together the pieces in each row. Press the seam allowances toward the sashing strips. Then join the rows. Press the seam allowances in one direction. The pieced quilt top should measure 58×73", including the seam allowances.

add the borders

1. Cut and piece seven white print 1¾×42" strips to make the following:
- 2—1¾×58" border strips
- 2—1¾×73" border strips

2. Aligning long raw edges, sew together one white print 1¾×42" strip and one light blue print 1¾×42" strip to make a strip set. Press the seam allowance toward the light blue strip. Repeat for a total of seven strip sets.

3. Cut a 1¾"-wide segment from a strip set. Repeat for a total of 152 segments. Combine two segments into a small Four-Patch unit in the same manner as before. Repeat to make a total of 76 light-blue-and-white small Four-Patch units.

4. For a top border unit you'll need 16 light-blue-and-white small Four-Patch units, six dark blue print C squares, two light blue print C squares, three light blue print D rectangles, eight dark blue print E rectangles, eight dark blue print F rectangles, four dark blue print G rectangles, and three dark blue print H rectangles.

5. Referring to Diagram 6, lay out the pieces for the top border unit. Sew together the pieces in vertical sections. Then join the sections. The pieced top border unit should measure 6¾×58", including seam allowances.

6. Sew one white print 1¾×58" border strip to the bottom edge of the top border unit. Join the border unit to the top edge of the pieced quilt top.

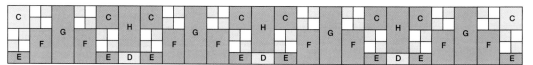

Diagram 6

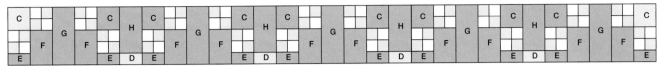

Diagram 8

7. Repeat steps 3 through 6 for the bottom border unit. Join the border unit to the bottom edge of the pieced quilt top.

8. For a corner block you'll need one light-blue-and-white small Four-Patch unit, one light blue print B rectangle, and two light blue print A rectangles.

9. Referring to Diagram 7 for placement, lay out the pieces as shown. Sew together the B rectangle and the small Four-Patch unit. Press the seam allowance toward the B rectangle. Then join the rows. Press the seam allowances in one direction. The pieced corner block should measure 8" square, including the seam allowances.

Diagram 7

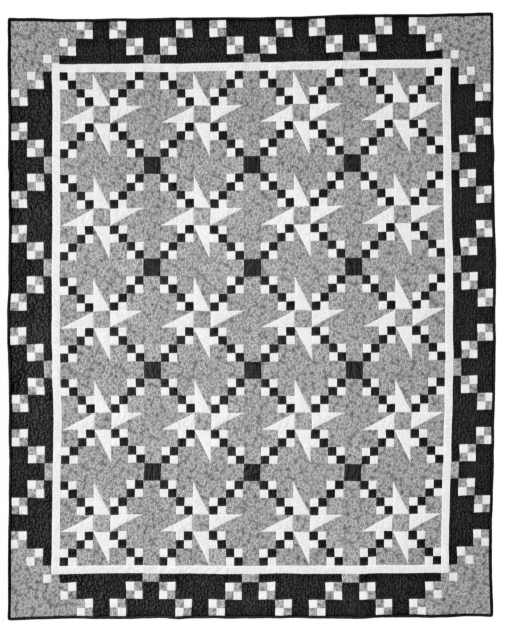

10. Repeat steps 8 and 9 to make a total of four corner blocks.

11. For a side border unit you'll need 20 light-blue-and-white small Four-Patch units, eight dark blue print C squares, two light blue print C squares, four light blue print D rectangles, 10 dark blue print E rectangles, 10 dark blue print F rectangles, five dark blue print G rectangles, and four dark blue print H rectangles.

12. Referring to Diagram 8, *page 55,* lay out the pieces for a side border unit. Sew together the pieces in vertical sections. Then join the sections. The pieced side border unit should measure 6¾×73", including seam allowances.

13. Sew one white print 1¾×73" border strip to the bottom edge of the side border unit. Add a corner block to each end of the side border unit. Join the border unit to one side edge of the pieced quilt top.

14. Repeat steps 11 through 13 for a second side border unit. Join the border unit to the remaining side edge of the pieced quilt top.

complete the quilt

Layer the quilt top, batting, and backing according to the instructions in Quilting Basics, which begins on page 94. Quilt as desired. Bind according to the instructions in Quilting Basics.

Snow Stars
Triangle

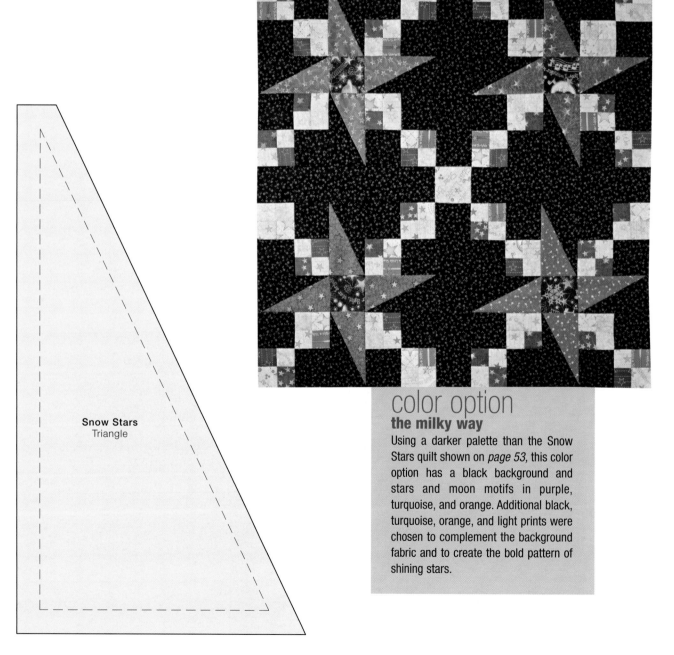

color option
the milky way

Using a darker palette than the Snow Stars quilt shown on *page 53,* this color option has a black background and stars and moon motifs in purple, turquoise, and orange. Additional black, turquoise, orange, and light prints were chosen to complement the background fabric and to create the bold pattern of shining stars.

beyond
basics

You've mastered straight and angled cuts and can cut around a template with ease. Now take your skills to the next level by learning to fussy-cut shapes, square up blocks, and trim away unwanted areas to round out your rotary-cutting skills.

jane's kaleidoscope

The drama of this single-shape quilt comes from the ornate floral fabrics rather than the piecing. Use clear templates to easily select and cut the fabric portions you wish to use.

Designer: Jane Sassaman   Photographer: Perry Struse

materials

Note: The yardages listed are liberal to allow for waste created by fussy cutting.

1 yard of purple begonia print (fabric 1) for blocks

1½ yards of yellow passionflower print (fabric 2) for blocks

1 yard of yellow-and-blue triflower print (fabric 3) for blocks

1⅓ yards of pink-and-green dahlia-and-daisy print (fabric 4) for blocks and border corners

1 yard of pink begonia print (fabric 5) for blocks

1 yard of purple passionflower print (fabric 6) for blocks

1 yard of yellow begonia print (fabric 7) for blocks

1 yard of pink passionflower print (fabric 8) for blocks

¾ yard of solid black for inner border and binding

¾ yard of willow leaf print for outer border

3⅛ yards of backing fabric

56×76" of quilt batting

Transparent template plastic

Tracing paper

Thread: black topstitching; black 50-weight cotton (optional)

FINISHED QUILT TOP: 50×70"

Quantities specified for 44/45"-wide, 100% cotton fabrics. All measurements include a ¼" seam allowance. Sew with right sides together unless otherwise stated.

cut the fabrics

To make the best use of your fabrics, cut the pieces in the order that follows. The patterns are on *page 60*. To make templates of the patterns, use transparent template plastic and follow the instructions in Quilting Basics, which begins on page 94.

from purple begonia print (fabric 1), cut:
- 3 of Pattern A
- 1 *each* of patterns B and B reversed

from yellow passionflower print (fabric 2), cut:
- 12 of Pattern A

from yellow-and-blue triflower print (fabric 3), cut:
- 8 of Pattern A

from pink-and-green dahlia-and-daisy print (fabric 4), cut:
- 6 of Pattern A
- 2 *each* of patterns B and B reversed
- 4—½" squares (Jane fussy-cut hers so each one would feature a large green daisy motif.)

from pink begonia print (fabric 5), cut:
- 3 of Pattern A
- 1 *each* of patterns B and B reversed

from purple passionflower print (fabric 6), cut:
- 3 of Pattern A
- 1 *each* of patterns B and B reversed

from yellow begonia print (fabric 7), cut:
- 4 of Pattern A

from pink passionflower print (fabric 8), cut:
- 3 of Pattern A
- 1 *each* of patterns B and B reversed

from solid black, cut:
- 6—2½×42" binding strips
- 5—1½×42" strips for inner border

designer notes

Isolating and cutting out a specific print motif is referred to as fussy cutting, which is how designer Jane Sassaman created this quilt's blooming, or kaleidoscope, effect. She used see-through triangle templates to determine which portion of a print she wanted to include, seeking symmetry within each triangle and repeating the same motif in all triangles cut from a fabric.

Jane suggests cutting several triangle patterns (A and B) from tracing paper and using them to experiment with placement. She also suggests marking the template placement with pins or chalk to make sure motifs align consistently within triangles from an individual fabric.

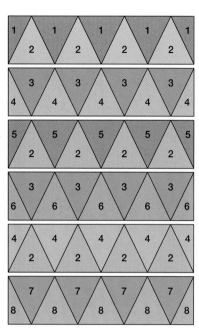

Quilt Assembly Diagram

from willow leaf print, cut:
- 6—4¹⁄₂×42" strips for outer border

assemble the quilt center

1. Referring to the Quilt Assembly Diagram, *left*, lay out the triangles in rows according to the fabric numbers.

2. Beginning with row 1, layer the first two triangles with adjoining long edges aligned; sew the adjoining long edges together. Press the seam allowance open.

3. Continue adding triangles to the first pair until the row is complete. The pieced row should measure 40¹⁄₂×10¹⁄₂", including the seam allowances.

4. Repeat steps 2 and 3 with each remaining row of triangles.

5. Layer rows 1 and 2 with adjoining long edges aligned; pin at the seam intersections. Join the rows. Press the seam allowance open.

6. Continue adding the remaining rows until all six are assembled into the quilt center; press the seam allowances open. The pieced quilt center should measure 40¹⁄₂×60¹⁄₂", including the seam allowances.

add the borders

1. Cut and piece the solid black 1¹⁄₂×42" strips to make the following:
- 2—1¹⁄₂×62¹⁄₂" inner border strips
- 2—1¹⁄₂×40¹⁄₂" inner border strips

2. With long edges aligned, sew the short solid black inner border strips to the top and bottom edges of the pieced quilt center. Then join the long solid black inner border strips to the side edges of the quilt center. Press all seam allowances toward the inner border.

3. Cut and piece the willow leaf print 4¹⁄₂×42" strips to make the following:
- 2—4¹⁄₂×62¹⁄₂" outer border strips
- 2—4¹⁄₂×42¹⁄₂" outer border strips

4. Sew the short willow leaf print outer border strips to the top and bottom edges of the pieced quilt center.

5. Join a pink-and-green dahlia-and-daisy print 4¹⁄₂" square to each end of the long willow leaf print outer border strips to make outer border units; press the seam allowances

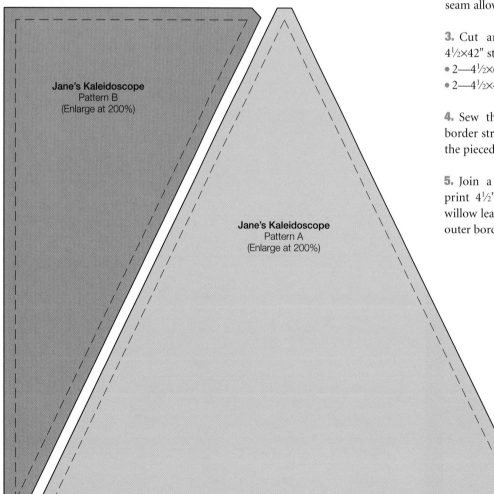

Jane's Kaleidoscope
Pattern B
(Enlarge at 200%)

Jane's Kaleidoscope
Pattern A
(Enlarge at 200%)

toward the pink-and-green print squares. *Note:* If the 4½" squares were fussy cut, make sure the motifs in the corners of the quilt will be mirror images of one another (see photograph, *below right*).

6. Sew the pieced outer border units to the side edges of the pieced quilt center to complete the quilt top. Press all seam allowances toward the outer border.

complete the quilt

1. Layer the quilt top, batting, and backing according to the instructions in Quilting Basics, which begins on page 94.

2. Quilt as desired. Jane used a simple wavy line design for her quilting pattern (see photograph, *below*), which she feels helps blend the quilt sections together. To get the length she desired, Jane taped together several pieces of template plastic and used a crafts knife to cut out a 1"-wide wavy strip.

"You can also go to your local office supply or party supply store and purchase a precut wavy party decoration to use instead," Jane says. Another option is to draw vertical wavy lines 1" apart on your quilt top.

Jane placed her wavy strip on her quilt top, marked the pattern with a light-color disappearing fabric marker, then machine-quilted the design with black topstitching thread in the machine's needle and black 50-weight cotton thread in the bobbin.

3. Use the solid black 2½×42" strips to bind the quilt according to the instructions in Quilting Basics.

town square picnic

Designer: Linda Hohag
Photographer: Perry Struse

Sharpen your rotary-cutting skills assembling this red, white, and blue salute to summer.

materials

1¾ yards of blue print for blocks, pieced border, and binding

1 yard of blue-and-white check for blocks and pieced border

⅞ yard of red print for blocks, inner border, and pieced border

2⅛ yards of solid white for blocks, middle border, and pieced border

3½ yards of backing fabric

61" square of quilt batting

FINISHED QUILT TOP: 54⅜" square
FINISHED BLOCK: 4¼" square

Quantities specified for 44/45"-wide, 100% cotton fabrics. All measurements include a ¼" seam allowance. Sew with right sides together unless otherwise stated.

cut the fabrics

To make the best use of your fabrics, cut the pieces in the order that follows.

The red print inner border strip measurements are mathematically correct. You may wish to cut your strips longer than specified to allow for possible sewing differences.

from blue print, cut:
- 6—2½×42" binding strips
- 8—1¼×42" strips
- 80—1¼×5" rectangles
- 28—3" squares
- 82—2" squares, cutting each in half diagonally for a total of 164 small triangles for block B

from blue-and-white check, cut:
- 4—3½×42" strips
- 13—4⅞" squares, cutting each diagonally twice in an X for a total of 52 large triangles for pieced border
- 6—2¾" squares, cutting each in half diagonally for a total of 12 corner triangles for pieced border

from red print, cut:
- 4—3½×42" strips
- 2—1¼×40¼" inner border strips
- 2—1¼×38¾" inner border strips
- 28—3" squares

from solid white, cut:
- 5—4¼×42" strips for middle border
- 8—1¼×42" strips
- 82—1¼×5" rectangles
- 13—4⅞" squares, cutting each diagonally twice in an X for a total of 52 large triangles for pieced border
- 2—2¾" squares, cutting each in half diagonally for a total of 4 corner triangles for pieced border
- 80—2" squares, cutting each in half diagonally for a total of 160 small triangles for block A

assemble the blocks

1. Aligning long edges, sew a blue print 1¼×42" strip to opposite sides of a blue-and-white check 3½×42" strip to make a strip set A (see Diagram 1). Press the seam allowances toward the blue print strips. Repeat to make a total of four of strip set A. Cut the strip sets into 3½" segments for a total of 40.

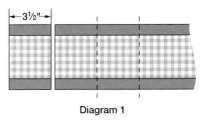

Diagram 1

2. Sew blue print 1¼×5" rectangles to opposite edges of a Step 1 segment to make a Unit A (see Diagram 2). Press the seam allowances toward the blue print rectangles. Pieced Unit A should measure 5" square, including the seam allowances. Repeat to make a total of 40 of Unit A.

Diagram 2

3. Lay a Unit A on point on a cutting mat. Position an acrylic ruler on the unit, aligning the ruler's 45° angle line along the unit's right-hand edge and leaving an accurate ¼" seam allowance beyond the right-hand point of the center square (see Diagram 3). With a

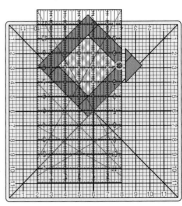

Diagram 3

rotary cutter, trim the right-hand edge of the block. Rotate the block and repeat the measuring, aligning, and trimming of each corner. Repeat with each Unit A.

4. Sew a solid white small triangle to each long edge of a Unit A to make a block A (see Diagram 4). Press the seam allowances toward the white triangles. Block A should measure 4¾" square, including the seam allowances.

Diagram 4

5. Repeat Step 4 to make a total of 40 of block A.

6. Using the solid white 1¼×42" strips and the red print 3½×42" strips, repeat Step 1 to make a total of four of strip set B (see Diagram 5). Cut the strip sets into 3½" segments for a total of 41.

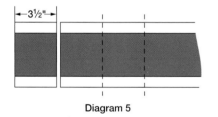

←—3½"—→

Diagram 5

7. Using the solid white 1¼×5" rectangles and the Step 6 segments, repeat Step 2 to make a total of 41 of Unit B (see Diagram 6).

Diagram 6

8. Repeat Step 3 to trim each of the 41 Unit Bs.

9. Using blue print small triangles and the trimmed Unit Bs, repeat Step 4 to make a total of 41 of block B (see Diagram 7). Press the seam allowances toward the blue print triangles. Block B should measure 4¾" square, including the seam allowances.

Diagram 7

assemble the quilt center

1. Referring to the photograph, *opposite,* lay out blocks A and B in nine horizontal rows, alternating blocks.

2. Sew together the blocks in each row. Press the seam allowances in one direction, alternating the direction with each row. Then join the rows to make the quilt center. Press the seam allowances in one direction. The pieced quilt center should measure 38¾" square, including the seam allowances.

add the borders

1. Sew the red print 1¼×38¾" inner border strips to opposite edges of the pieced quilt center. Then join the red print 1¼×40¼" inner border strips to the remaining edges of the quilt center. Press the seam allowances toward the red print inner border.

2. Cut and piece the solid white 4¼×42" strips to make the following:
• 2—4¼×47¾" middle border strips
• 2—4¼×40¼" middle border strips

3. Sew the short solid white middle border strips to opposite edges of the pieced quilt center. Then join the long solid white middle border strips to the remaining edges of the

pieced quilt center. Press the seam allowances toward the red print inner border. Trim the pieced quilt center to measure 47⅝" square, including the seam allowances.

4. Referring to Diagram 8, sew together a red print 3" square, a blue-and-white check large triangle, and a solid white large triangle to make a red print Unit C. Press the seam allowances toward the red print square. Repeat to make a total of 24 of red print Unit C.

Diagram 8

5. Referring to Diagram 9 and repeating Step 4, use blue print 3" squares, blue-and-white check large triangles, and solid white large triangles to make a total of 24 of blue print Unit C.

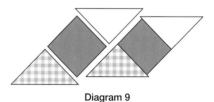

Diagram 9

6. Referring to Diagram 10, join a solid white large triangle and a blue print 3" square to make a blue print Unit D. Repeat to make a second blue print Unit D.

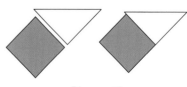

Diagram 10

7. Referring to Diagram 11 and repeating Step 6, use red print 3" squares and solid white large triangles to make a total of two of red print Unit D.

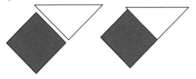

Diagram 11

8. Referring to Diagram 12, join a blue-and-white check large triangle and a blue print 3" square to make a blue print Unit E.

Diagram 12

Repeat to make a second blue print Unit E. In the same manner, join a red print 3" square and a blue-and-white check large triangle to make a red print Unit E (see Diagram 13). Repeat to make a second red print Unit E.

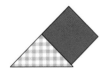

Diagram 13

9. Referring to Diagram 14, lay out six of red print Unit C, five of blue print Unit C, one blue print Unit D, one blue print Unit E, two solid white corner triangles, and two blue-and-white check corner triangles. Sew together the units to make a short pieced outer border strip. Press the seam allowances in one direction. The short pieced outer border strip should measure $4\frac{1}{8}\times47\frac{5}{8}$" including the seam allowances. Repeat to make a second short pieced outer border strip.

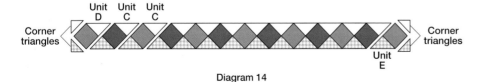

Diagram 14

10. Referring to Diagram 15, lay out six of red print Unit C, seven of blue print Unit C, one red print Unit D, one red print Unit E, and four blue-and-white check corner triangles. Sew together the units to make a long pieced outer border strip. Press the seam allowances in one direction. The long pieced outer border strip should measure $4\frac{1}{8}\times54\frac{7}{8}$" including the seam allowances. Repeat to make a second long pieced outer border strip.

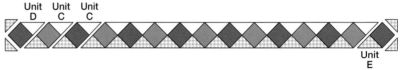

Diagram 15

11. Referring to the photograph on *page 64*, for placement, sew the short pieced outer border strips to opposite edges of the quilt center. Then add the long pieced outer border strips to the remaining edges of the quilt center to complete the quilt top. Press the seam allowances toward the middle border.

complete the quilt

1. Layer the quilt top, batting, and backing according to the instructions in Quilting Basics, which begins on page 94.

2. Quilt as desired. Machine-quilter Heather Mulder quilted a four-petal flower motif in the center of each block and rows of flowers and stems in the white middle border. She did an allover stipple in the remainder of the quilt center and in the blue-and-white check pieces of the pieced outer border. She did not quilt in the red print and blue print squares of the pieced outer border.

3. Use the blue print $2\frac{1}{2}\times42$" strips to bind the quilt according to the instructions in Quilting Basics.

color option
perk it up!

Although the patriotic version of Town Square Picnic shown on *page 63* is bright and colorful, this wall-size color option gets an equal jolt of color in blacks, browns, golds, blues, and reds.

Instead of white fabric, this version uses a black coffee bean print as the main color. Thoughtful placement of lights and darks makes the blocks with less contrast recede and those with more contrast appear to pop out.

slice &dice

Sit and sew now, and square up blocks later with this fast and fun piecing method.

Designer: Mabeth Oxenreider
Photographer: Perry Struse

materials

10—¼-yard pieces of assorted dark batiks for blocks

10—¼-yard pieces of assorted light batiks for blocks

¼ yard of solid orange for inner border

1½ yards of purple print for outer border and binding

2⅞ yards of backing fabric

52" square of quilt batting

6½"-square see-through acrylic ruler (optional)

FINISHED QUILT TOP: 46" square
FINISHED BLOCK: 4" square

Quantities specified for 44/45"-wide, 100% cotton fabrics. All measurements include a ¼" seam allowance. Sew with right sides together unless otherwise stated.

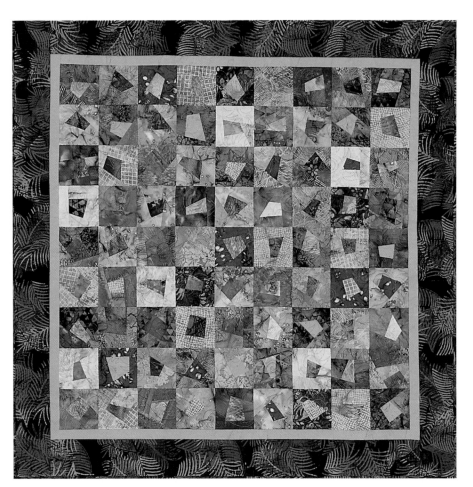

cut the fabrics

To make the best use of your fabrics, cut the pieces in the order that follows. The outer border strips are cut lengthwise (parallel to the selvage). The measurements are mathematically correct. You may wish to cut your strips longer than specified to allow for possible sewing differences.

from assorted dark batiks, cut:

- 164—2½×5" rectangles in sets of four (you'll have a total of 41 sets)

from assorted light batiks, cut:

- 160—2½×5" rectangles in sets of four (you'll have a total of 40 sets)

from solid orange, cut:

- 2—1½×38½" inner border strips
- 2—1½×36½" inner border strips

from purple print, cut:

- 5—2½×42" binding strips
- 2—4½×46½" outer border strips
- 2—4½×38½" outer border strips

assemble the blocks

1. From a light batik scrap cut an asymmetrical, four-sided piece for a block center. (The edges of the center pieces in the quilt on *page 67* range from 1½" to 3½".) Repeat to cut a total of 41 light batik block centers and 40 dark batik block centers in varying sizes.

2. Place a light batik block center facedown on the center of a dark batik 2½×5" rectangle. Referring to Diagram 1, sew together along a long edge. Press the pieces open (see Diagram 2).

Diagram 1   Diagram 2

3. Referring to Diagram 3, position a dark batik 2½×5" rectangle from the same set on the pieced unit and sew together. Press open as before (see Diagram 4).

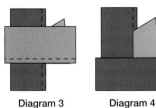

Diagram 3   Diagram 4

4. Repeat the process with the remaining dark batik 2½×5" rectangles in the set, joining them to the remaining raw edges of the block center and pressing open (see Diagram 5).

Diagram 5

5. Place the 6½" square acrylic ruler over the pieced unit at any angle (see Diagram 6) and trim it to 4½" square to make a dark batik block.

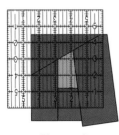

Diagram 6

6. Repeat steps 2 through 5 to make a total of 41 dark batik blocks.

7. Repeat steps 2 through 5 using the light batik 2½×5" rectangles and the dark batik block centers to make a total of 40 light batik blocks.

assemble the quilt center

1. Referring to the photograph, *opposite,* for placement, lay out the 41 dark batik blocks and the 40 light batik blocks in nine horizontal rows, alternating light and dark blocks.

2. Sew together the blocks in each row. Press the seam allowances in one direction, alternating directions with each row. Then join the rows to make the quilt center. Press the seam allowances in one direction. The quilt center should measure 36½" square, including the seam allowances.

add the borders

1. Sew the solid orange 1½×36½" inner border strips to opposite edges of the pieced quilt center. Then join the solid orange 1½×38½" inner border strips to the remaining edges of the pieced quilt center. Press all the seam allowances toward the border.

2. Sew the purple print 4½×38½" outer border strips to opposite edges of the pieced quilt center. Then join the purple print 4½×46½" outer border strips to the remaining edges of the pieced quilt center to complete the quilt top. Press all the seam allowances toward the outer border.

complete the quilt

1. Layer the quilt top, batting, and backing according to the instructions in Quilting Basics, which begins on page 94. Quilt as desired.

2. Use the purple print 2½×42" strips to bind the quilt according to the instructions in Quilting Basics.

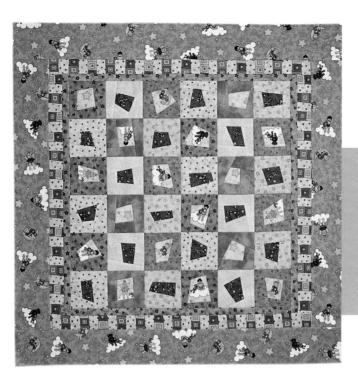

color option
oh baby!

Even though this crib-size quilt is smaller than the original "Slice & Dice" project, *page 67,* that's no reason to shy away from large-scale prints. This color option in greens and pinks was created by fussy-cutting about half of the block centers, centering a motif in the block. The large-motif fabric is repeated in the borders as well.

Optional Size Chart for Slice & Dice			
ALTERNATE QUILT SIZES	**TWIN**	**FULL/QUEEN**	**KING**
Number of Dark Batik Blocks	124	200	265
Number of Light Batik Blocks	123	199	264
Number of Blocks Wide by Long	13×19	19×21	23×23
Finished Size	62×86"	86×94"	102" square
YARDAGE REQUIREMENTS			
Total yards of assorted dark batiks	7¾ yards	12½ yards	16¾ yards
Total yards of assorted light batiks	7¾ yards	12½ yards	16½ yards
Solid orange for inner border	⅜ yard	½ yard	⅝ yard
Purple print for outer border			
and binding	2⅓ yards	2⅝ yards	3 yards
Backing fabric	5⅛ yards	7⅔ yards	9 yards
Batting	68×92"	92×100"	108" square

*Note: The method used for making this quilt requires that an unusually large amount of fabric is wasted as the blocks are trimmed to size. Save the scraps from this project for use on another scrap quilt.

■ rotary-cutting
primer

With a rotary cutter you can make accurate cuts through multiple layers of fabric. One of the strongest appeals of rotary cutting is the precision and speed with which you can cut multiple strips, squares, triangles, and diamonds, thus enhancing your enjoyment of the quiltmaking process.

As with many techniques, the more you practice the easier and more natural the process will become. Practice rotary cutting on fabric scraps until you develop confidence in your cutting accuracy.

tool basics

To rotary-cut fabrics you need three basic pieces of equipment—a rotary cutter, acrylic ruler, and cutting mat.

A rotary cutter should always be used with a cutting mat designed specifically for rotary cutting. The mat protects the cutting surface and keeps the fabric from shifting while it's being cut.

Cutting mats usually have one side printed with a grid and one side that's plain. To avoid confusion when lining up fabric with the lines printed on the ruler, some quilters prefer to use the plain side of the mat. Others prefer to use the mat's grid.

The round blade of a rotary cutter is razor sharp. Because of this, be sure to use a cutter with a safety guard and keep the guard over the blade whenever you're not cutting. Rotary cutters are commonly available in three sizes; a good all-purpose blade is a 45 mm.

fabric grain

Always consider the fabric grain before cutting. The arrow on the pattern piece or template indicates which direction the fabric grain should run. Because one or more straight sides of every fabric piece should follow the lengthwise or crosswise grain, it is important that the line on the pattern or template runs parallel to the grain.

The lengthwise grain runs parallel to the tightly woven finished edge, or selvage, and is sometimes referred to as the straight grain. It has the least amount of stretch and is the strongest and smoothest grain. Do not use the selvage edge in a quilt. When washed, the selvage, because it is so tightly woven, may shrink more than the rest of the fabric.

The crosswise grain runs perpendicular to the selvage. It is sometimes referred to as the cross grain. The crosswise grain is usually looser and has slightly more stretch than the lengthwise grain.

True bias intersects the lengthwise grain and crosswise grain at a 45° angle, but any line that runs diagonally between the two grain lines is called the bias. It has more stretch and flexibility than either the crosswise or lengthwise grain.

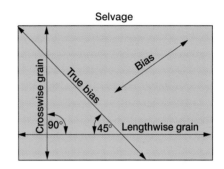

When the lengthwise grain and the crosswise grain intersect at a perfect right angle, the fabric is said to be on grain, or grain perfect. If the grains don't intersect at a perfect right angle, they are considered off grain and the threads are distorted.

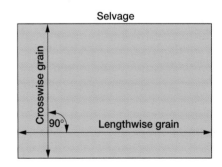

A fabric that is slightly off grain is still usable. However, significantly off-grain fabric will require careful handling during assembly and heavy quilting to stabilize it in a finished quilt.

squaring up the fabric edge

Before rotary-cutting fabric into strips, it is imperative that one edge of the fabric be straightened, or squared up. Since the accuracy of all subsequent cuts depends on this first cut, squaring up the fabric edge is a critical step. There are several ways to square up fabric, but here we show two common ways: the single-ruler technique and the double-ruler technique.

squaring up with the single-ruler technique

This method requires just one ruler, but you must turn the mat or move to the opposite side of your cutting surface after squaring up the fabric before you can begin cutting strips.

1. Lay the fabric right side down on your cutting mat with one selvage edge away from you.

2. Fold the fabric in half with the wrong side inside and selvages together.

3. Fold the fabric in half again, aligning the folded edge with the selvage edges. Lightly hand-crease all folds.

4. Position the folded fabric on the cutting mat with selvage edges away from you and the bulk of the fabric to your left.

5. With ruler on top of fabric, align a horizontal grid line on the ruler with the lower folded fabric edge, leaving about 1" of fabric exposed along the right-hand edge of ruler.

Do not try to align the uneven raw edges along the other side of the fabric. If the grid lines on the cutting mat interfere with your ability to focus on the ruler grid lines, turn your cutting mat over and work on the unmarked side.

6. Hold ruler firmly in place with your left hand, spreading your fingers apart slightly and keeping them away from the right-hand edge of the ruler. Apply pressure to the ruler with fingertips. (Some quilters keep their little finger just off the ruler edge, pressing it on the cutting mat to stabilize the ruler.) With the ruler firmly in

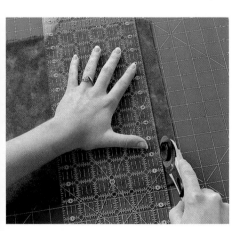

place, hold the rotary cutter with the handle at an angle to the cutting mat and the blade abutted against the ruler's right-hand edge. Roll the blade along the ruler's edge, starting your cut just off the folded edge and pushing the cutter away from you, toward the selvage edges.

7. The fabric strip to the right of the ruler's edge should be cut cleanly away, leaving you with a straight edge from which you can measure all subsequent cuts. Do not pick up the fabric once the edge has been squared; instead, turn the cutting mat to rotate the fabric.

8. Begin cutting strips, measuring from the cut edge.

cutting several strips in succession

When cutting several fabric strips in succession, it is possible for your ruler to get slightly askew, causing your strips to be crooked. How will you know? When you open a strip, there will be a slight swerve or bump at the center fold line.

To avoid cutting multiple crooked strips, stop every few strips when you're cutting and open them up. If you discover a bump in the middle, square up your fabric again before cutting any more strips.

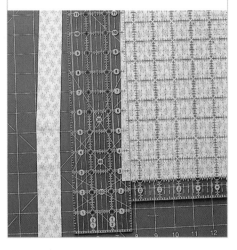

squaring up with the two-ruler technique

This method requires two rulers, but you can begin cutting strips as soon as the fabric is squared up; turning the mat is not necessary.

1. Lay the fabric right side down on your cutting mat with one selvage edge away from you.

2. Fold the fabric in half with the wrong side inside and selvages together.

3. Fold the fabric in half again, aligning the folded edge with the selvage edges. Lightly hand-crease all the folds.

4. Position the folded fabric on the cutting mat with selvage edges away from you and the bulk of the fabric to your right.

5. With a large square ruler on top of the fabric, align a horizontal grid line on the ruler with the lower folded fabric edge. Leave a small amount of fabric exposed along the left-hand edge of the ruler. About a rectangular ruler against the square ruler along left-hand edge.

6. Carefully remove the large square ruler, leaving the rectangular ruler in place.

7. Trim away the edge of the fabric to square up fabric. Do not pick up the fabric once the edge has been squared.

8. Reposition the rectangular ruler and you're ready to begin cutting strips, measuring from the cut edge without rotating the cutting mat.

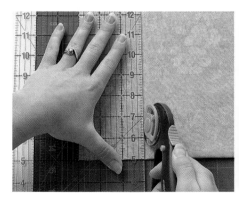

cutting fabric wider than the ruler

Occasionally you'll need to cut fabric that is wider than the ruler is long. Cutting border strips from the lengthwise grain is one example.

1. After squaring up the fabric, align the ruler and cut to the end of the ruler (see page 72 for instructions on squaring up the fabric edge).

2. Leaving rotary cutter in place on the fabric, slide the ruler ahead to the uncut area. Align the ruler edge with the fabric's cut edge.

3. Continue cutting and moving the ruler ahead as needed until the desired length of fabric has been cut.

QUICK REFERENCE CHART
YARDAGE ESTIMATOR: SQUARES FROM STRIPS

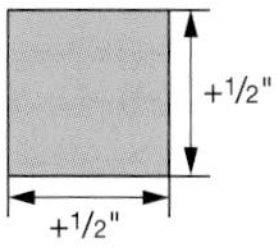

Use this chart to determine the number of squares that can be cut from various yardages. The figures on this chart are mathematically accurate. You may want to purchase extra fabric to allow for errors.

Yardage figures include ¼" seam allowances and are based on 42"-long strips.

SIZE OF SQUARE		YARDAGE (44/45"-wide fabric)							
Finished	Cut Strip Width	¼	½	¾	1	1¼	1½	1¾	2
1"	1½"	168	336	504	672	840	1008	1176	1344
1½"	2"	84	189	273	378	462	567	651	756
2"	2½"	48	112	160	224	288	336	400	448
2½"	3"	42	84	126	168	210	252	294	336
3"	3½"	24	60	84	120	144	180	216	240
3½"	4"	20	40	60	90	110	130	150	180
4"	4½"	18	36	54	72	90	108	126	144
4½"	5"	8	24	40	56	72	80	96	112
5"	5½"	7	21	28	42	56	63	77	91
5½"	6"	7	21	28	42	49	63	70	84
6"	6½"	6	12	24	30	36	48	54	66
6½"	7"	6	12	18	30	36	42	54	60
7"	7½"	5	10	15	20	30	35	40	45
7½"	8"	5	10	15	20	25	30	35	45
8"	8½"	4	8	12	16	20	24	28	32
8½"	9"	4	8	12	16	20	24	28	32
9"	9½"	-	4	8	12	16	20	24	28
9½"	10"	-	4	8	12	16	20	24	28
10"	10½"	-	4	8	12	16	20	24	24
10½"	11"	-	3	6	9	12	12	15	18
11"	11½"	-	3	6	9	9	12	15	18
11½"	12"	-	3	6	9	9	12	15	18
12"	12½"	-	3	6	6	9	12	15	15
12½"	13"	-	3	6	6	9	12	12	15
13"	13½"	-	3	6	6	9	12	12	15
13½"	14"	-	3	3	6	9	9	12	15
14"	14½"	-	2	2	4	6	6	8	8
14½"	15"	-	2	2	4	6	6	8	8
15"	15½"	-	2	2	4	4	6	8	8
15½"	16"	-	2	2	4	4	6	6	8
16"	16½"	-	2	2	4	4	6	6	8
16½"	17"	-	2	2	4	4	6	6	8
17"	17½"	-	2	2	4	4	6	6	8
18"	18½"	-	-	2	2	4	4	6	6

YARDAGE ESTIMATOR: RECTANGLES FROM STRIPS

Use this chart to determine the number of rectangles that can be cut from various yardages (see note below on cutting strip width for rectangles). *Yardage figures include ¼" seam allowances and are based on 42"-long strips.*

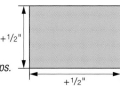

SIZE OF RECTANGLES		YARDAGE (44/45"-wide fabric)							
Finished	Cut Strip Width	¼	½	¾	1	1¼	1½	1¾	2
1×2"	1½×2½"	96	*196	288	*392	*504	*588	*700	*784
1×3"	1½×3½"	72	144	216	288	360	432	504	576
1½×3"	2×3½"	48	108	156	216	264	324	*378	432
1½×4½"	2×5"	32	72	*105	*147	*189	216	*252	*294
1½×8"	2×8½"	*21	*42	*63	*84	*105	*126	*147	*168
1½×9"	2×9½"	16	36	52	72	88	108	*126	*147
1½×10"	2×10½"	16	36	52	72	88	108	*126	144
1½×12"	2×12½"	12	27	*42	54	66	*84	*105	108
2×4"	2½×4½"	*32	*64	*96	*128	162	*192	225	*256
2×6"	2½×6½"	18	42	*64	84	108	*128	150	*176
2×8"	2½×8½"	*16	*32	*48	*64	*80	*96	*112	*128
2×9"	2½×9½"	12	28	40	56	72	84	100	112
2×10"	2½×10½"	12	28	40	56	72	84	100	112
2×12"	2½×12½"	9	21	*32	42	54	*64	*80	84
2½×5"	3×5½"	21	42	63	84	*112	126	*154	*182
2½×7½"	3×8"	15	30	45	60	75	90	105	*126
2½×8"	3×8½"	*14	*28	*42	*56	*70	*84	*98	*112
2½×9"	3×9½"	12	24	36	48	60	72	84	*98
2½×10"	3×10½"	12	24	36	48	60	72	84	96
2½×12"	3×12½"	9	18	*28	36	45	*56	*70	72
3×6"	3½×6½"	12	30	*48	60	72	*96	108	*132
3×8"	3½×8½"	*12	*24	*36	*48	*60	*72	*84	*96
3×9"	3½×9½"	8	20	28	40	48	60	72	*84
3×10"	3½×10½"	8	20	28	40	48	60	72	80
3×12"	3½×12½"	6	15	*24	30	36	*48	*60	60

*Note: Unless otherwise noted, always cut your initial strip from the smallest width of the rectangle. Sometimes you will reap more pieces from your yardage if you cut the first strip at the larger width. These exceptions have been denoted with an asterisk (*). For example, follow the line to the right of "Finished 1×2", Cut Strip Width 1½×2½"." With ½ yard of fabric, you will get more rectangles if you first cut strips 2½", then cross-cut the strips into 1½" segments.

cutting squares or rectangles from strips

Use a rotary cutter and strips of fabric to cut multiple squares and rectangles accurately and quickly.

1. To cut squares, cut fabric strips that are the desired finished measurement of the square, plus ½" for seam allowances. For example, for 3" finished squares, cut 3½"-wide fabric strips.

2. Square up one end of each strip (see page 72 for instructions).

3. Using a ruler, align a vertical grid line with the cut edge of a fabric strip. Align the top and bottom edges of fabric strip with horizontal lines on ruler.

To cut squares, cut fabric into lengths equal to the strip width. For example, for 3" finished squares, cut the 3½"-wide fabric strips into 3½"-long pieces.

4. To cut rectangles, cut fabric strips that are the desired finished length, plus ½" for seam allowances. For example, for 3×5" finished rectangles, cut 3½"-wide fabric strips into 5½" lengths.

cutting a single square or rectangle

1. Align a ruler in a fabric corner. Make two cuts along the ruler's edges to separate the section from remainder of fabric. Make sure the section is slightly larger than the square or rectangle you need.

2. Rotate the section of fabric and align the cut edges of fabric with the desired measurements on the ruler. Make two more cuts along the ruler's edges to complete the square or rectangle.

fussy cutting

Isolating and cutting out a specific print or pattern is referred to as fussy cutting.

1. Trace finished-size shape on a piece of frosted template plastic that is at least 2" larger on all sides than desired shape.

2. Using a crafts knife and ruler, cut away the interior of the shape to make a viewing window.

3. Move the viewing window over the fabric to isolate the desired portion of the print. Mark position with pins or chalk.

4. Remove the viewing window and re-mark as needed. Add seam allowances and cut out the print portion with scissors or a rotary cutter and ruler.

cutting half-square triangles

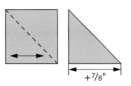

+⁷/₈"

1. Square up the fabric (see page 72 for instructions).

2. Cut the fabric in strips as wide as the desired finished width of the triangle-squares, plus ⁷/₈" for seam allowances. For example, for a 3" finished half-square triangle, cut a 3⅞"-wide fabric strip.

3. Square up one end of each strip.

4. Using a ruler, cut the strip into lengths equal to the strip's width. In this example, the strip would be cut into 3⅞"-long pieces.

5. Position the ruler diagonally across a square and cut the square in half to make two equal-size right triangles.

QUICK REFERENCE CHART
YARDAGE ESTIMATOR: FLYING GEESE AND SQUARES FROM STRIPS

If you're using the one rectangle and two squares method of making Flying Geese units, use this chart to determine the number of rectangles and squares that can be cut from various yardages (see note below on cutting strip width for rectangles).

Yardage figures include ¼" seam allowances and are based on 42"-long strips.

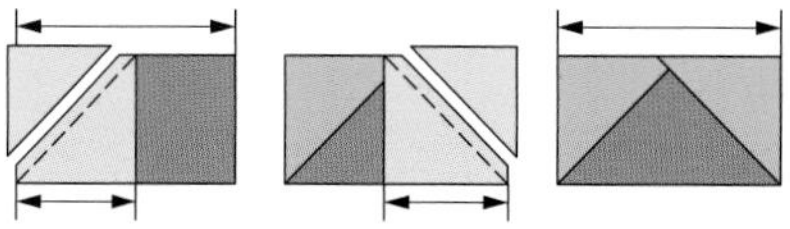

SIZE OF RECTANGLES AND SQUARES				YARDAGE (44/45"-wide fabric)							
Finished Unit Size	Rectangle Size	Square Size	Cut Strip Width	¼	½	¾	1	1¼	1½	1¾	2
½×1"	1×1½"		1"*	252	504	756	1,008	1,260	1,512	1,764	2,016
		1"	1"	378	756	1,134	1,512	1,890	2,268	2,646	3,024
¾×1½"	1¼×2"		1¼"*	147	*297	441	*594	756	903	1,050	1,197
		1¼"	1¼"	231	462	693	924	1,188	1,419	1,650	1,881
1×2"	1½×2½"		1½"*	96	*196	288	*392	480	*588	*700	*784
		1½"	1½"	168	336	504	672	840	1,008	1,176	1,344
1¼×2½"	1¾×3"		1¾"*	*72	*144	*216	*288	*360	*432	504	*576
		1¾"	1¾"	120	240	360	480	600	720	864	984
1½×3"	2×3½"		2"*	48	108	156	216	264	324	*378	432
		2"	2"	84	189	273	378	462	567	651	756
1¾×3½"	2¼×4"		2¼"*	40	80	120	*162	200	240	280	*324
		2¼"	2¼"	72	144	216	288	360	432	504	576
2×4"	2½×4½"		2½"*	*32	*64	*96	*128	162	*192	225	*256
		2½"	2½"	48	112	160	224	288	336	400	448
2¼×4½"	2¾×5"		2¾"*	24	48	*75	*105	*135	152	*180	*210
		2¾"	2¾"	45	90	135	195	240	285	330	390
2½×5"	3×5½"		3"*	21	42	63	84	*112	126	*154	*182
		3"	3"	42	84	126	168	210	252	294	336
2¾×5½"	3¼×6"		3¼"*	14	*36	56	77	91	112	133	154
		3¼"	3¼"	24	60	96	132	156	192	228	264
3×6"	3½×6½"		3½"*	12	30	*48	60	72	*96	108	*132
		3½"	3½"	24	60	84	120	144	180	216	240
3¼×6½"	3¾×7"		3¾"*	12	24	42	*55	72	84	*99	114
		3¾"	3¾"	22	44	77	99	132	154	176	209
3½×7"	4×7½"		4"*	10	20	30	45	*60	*70	*80	90
		4"	4"	20	40	60	90	110	130	150	180
3¾×7½"	4¼×8"		4¼"*	10	20	30	40	50	60	70	*81
		4¼"	4¼"	18	36	54	72	90	108	126	144
4×8"	4½×8½"		4½"*	8	*18	*27	*36	*45	*54	*63	*72
		4½"	4½"	18	36	54	72	90	108	126	144

*Note: Unless otherwise noted, always cut your initial strip from the smallest width of the rectangle. Sometimes you'll reap more pieces from yardage if you cut the first strip at the larger width. These exceptions are denoted with an asterisk (*). For example, follow the line to the right of "Finished Unit Size 1×2", Rectangle Size 1½×2½", Cut Strip Width 1½"." With ½ yard of fabric, you'll get more rectangles if you first cut strips 2½", then cross-cut the strips into 1½" segments.

YARDAGE ESTIMATOR: QUARTER-SQUARE (RIGHT) TRIANGLES FROM STRIPS

Use this chart to determine the number of quarter-square triangles that can be cut from various yardages.

Yardage figures include ¼" seam allowances and are based on 42"-long strips.

SIZE OF TRIANGLE		YARDAGE (44/45"-wide fabric)							
Finished	Cut Strip Width	¼	½	¾	1	1¼	1½	1¾	2
1"	2¼"	288	576	864	1,152	1,440	1,728	2,016	2,304
1½"	2¾"	180	360	540	780	960	1,140	1,320	1,560
2"	3¼"	96	240	384	528	624	768	912	1,056
2½"	3¾"	88	176	308	396	528	616	704	836
3"	4¼"	72	144	216	288	360	432	504	576
3½"	4¾"	32	96	160	224	288	352	416	480
4"	5¼"	32	96	160	192	256	320	384	416
4½"	5¾"	28	84	112	168	196	252	280	336
5"	6¼"	24	48	96	120	168	192	240	264
5½"	6¾"	24	48	96	120	144	192	216	240
6"	7¼"	20	40	60	80	120	140	160	180
6½"	7¾"	20	40	60	80	100	120	160	180
7"	8¼"	20	40	60	80	100	120	140	160
7½"	8¾"	16	32	48	64	80	96	112	128
8"	9¼"	-	16	32	48	64	80	96	112
8½"	9¾"	-	16	32	48	64	80	96	112
9"	10¼"	-	16	32	48	64	80	96	112
9½"	10¾"	-	12	24	36	48	60	60	72
10"	11¼"	-	12	24	36	48	48	60	72
10½"	11¾"	-	12	24	36	36	48	60	72
11"	12¼"	-	12	24	24	36	48	60	60
11½"	12¾"	-	12	24	24	36	48	48	60
12"	13¼"	-	12	24	24	36	48	48	60
12½"	13¾"	-	12	12	24	36	36	48	60
13"	14¼"	-	8	8	16	24	24	32	40
13½"	14¾"	-	8	8	16	24	24	32	32
14"	15¼"	-	8	8	16	16	24	32	32
14½"	15¾"	-	8	8	16	16	24	32	32
15"	16¼"	-	8	8	16	16	24	24	32
15½"	16¾"	-	8	8	16	16	24	24	32
16"	17¼"	-	8	8	16	16	24	24	32
16½"	17¾"	-	8	8	16	16	24	24	32
17"	18¼"	-	-	8	8	16	16	24	24
18"	19¼"	-	-	8	8	16	16	24	24

cutting quarter-square triangles

1. Square up the fabric (see page 72 for instructions).

2. Cut the fabric in strips as wide as the desired finished width of the quarter-square triangle, plus 1¼" for seam allowances. For example, for a 3" finished quarter-square triangle, cut a 4¼"-wide fabric strip.

3. Square up one end of each strip.

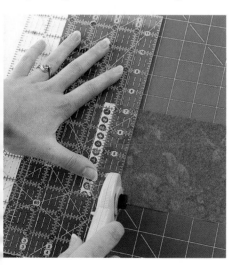

4. Using a ruler, cut the strip into lengths equal to the strip's width. In this example, the strip would be cut into 4¼"-long pieces.

5. Position the ruler diagonally across square and cut the square in half to make two equal-size right triangles. Do not move or pick up the triangles.

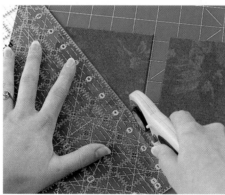

6. Position the ruler diagonally across the cut square in the opposite direction and cut the square in half again to make a total of four equal-size triangles.

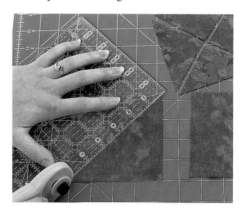

rotary-cutting tips

- You can rotary-cut more than one large piece of fabric at a time. For best results, layer only up to four pieces. More than four layers may mean less precision.

- Before rotary-cutting, use spray sizing or spray starch to stabilize the large fabric pieces.

- Press to temporarily hold the fabric layers together.

cutting center triangles for isosceles triangle-in-a-square blocks

+7/8"

The center triangle in a triangle-in-a-square block is an isosceles triangle, which means it has two sides of equal length.

1. Square up the fabric (see page 72 for instructions).

2. Cut the fabric in strips as wide as the desired finished width of the triangle, plus 7/8". For example, to make an isosceles triangle for a 3" finished triangle-in-a-square, cut a 3⅞"-wide fabric strip.

3. Square up one end of each strip.

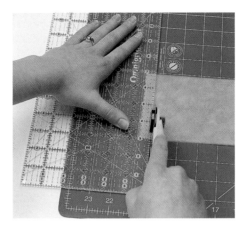

4. Position the ruler over the strip and cut a square. In this example, cut a 3⅞" square from the 3⅞"-wide strip.

5. Fold the square in half to find top center and lightly finger-crease.

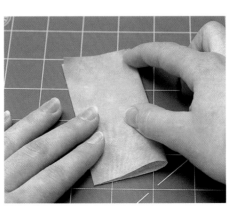

6. Position ruler diagonally across the square from a bottom corner to the creased top center mark and cut. Do not pick up the fabric pieces.

7. Rotate the ruler only and align it diagonally from the other bottom corner to the creased top center mark and cut.

cutting side triangles for isosceles triangle-in-a-square blocks

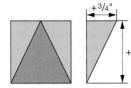

The side triangles in a triangle-in-a-square block are long triangles with a 90° corner.

1. Square up the fabric (see page 72 for instructions).

2. Cut the fabric in strips as wide as the desired finished width of the side triangle plus ¾". For example, for a 3" finished triangle-in-a-square, the finished width of the side triangle is 1½", so you would cut a 2¼"-wide fabric strip (1½" + ¾").

3. Position two layers of strips, stacked with like sides together, parallel to one of the mat's grid lines and square up one end.

4. Position the ruler over the stacked strips and measure the desired finished height of the side triangle, plus 1¼" for seam allowances, and cut the rectangle. In this example, make one cut in the stacked 2¼"-wide strips to make two rectangles each 2¼×4¼".

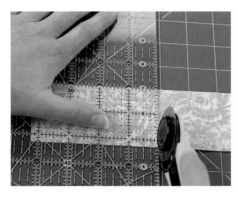

Note: The isosceles triangle-in-a-square has two side triangles that are mirror images of each other. Always cut in double layers to make the mirror-image shapes. Two rectangles yield two left-hand side triangles and two right-hand side triangles.

5. Position the ruler diagonally across the stacked rectangles and cut the rectangles in half to make two each of the left-hand and right-hand side triangles.

tip When aligning the pieces to sew together an isosceles triangle-in-a-square block, the side triangles must be even with the top point of the center triangle. The dog-ears extend at the base of the center triangle.

Once sewn together, this overlap at the top of the triangle is what creates the seam allowance along the upper edge of the block. When you sew it to another block, this seam allowance will be taken in, leaving the tip of your center triangle intact at the seam line.

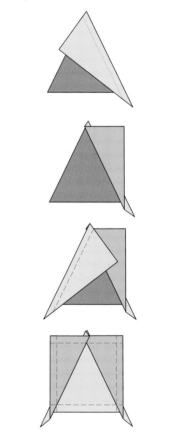

cutting 45° trapezoids

1. Square up the fabric (see page 72 for instructions).

2. Cut the fabric in strips as wide as the desired finished height of the trapezoid, plus ½" for seam allowances. For example, for a 3"-high trapezoid, cut a 3½"-wide fabric strip.

3. Square up one end of each strip.

4. Position the ruler over a strip and measure the desired finished length of the trapezoid, plus 1¼" for seam allowances, and cut a rectangle. For example, for a 10¼"-long finished trapezoid, cut an 11½" length from the strip to make a 3½×11½" rectangle.

5. Align a ruler's 45° line with the horizontal edge of the rectangle. Cut a 45° angle from the bottom corner to the top edge. Do not pick up the fabric rectangle.

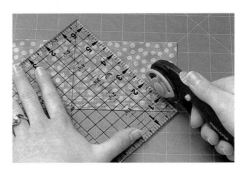

6. Pick up and rotate the ruler only. Position it on the opposite rectangle end and align the 45° line with the opposite edge of the fabric. Cut a 45° angle from the bottom corner to the top edge.

cutting 45° diamonds

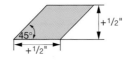

1. Square up the fabric (see page 72 for instructions).

2. Cut the fabric in strips as wide as the desired finished width of the diamond, plus ½" for seam allowances. For example, for a 3"-wide diamond, cut a 3½"-wide fabric strip.

3. Square up one end of each strip.

4. Position the ruler on the strip, aligning the 45° line with the horizontal edge of the strip. Cut a 45° angle from the bottom edge to the top edge.

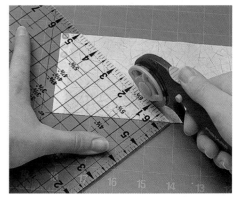

5. Aligning the ruler with the first cut edge, reposition the ruler on the strip at the desired width measurement, plus ½" for seam allowances. Cut a second 45° angle parallel to the first from the bottom edge to the top edge.

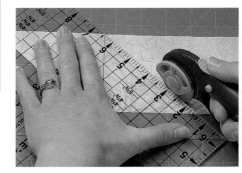

cutting 60° equilateral triangles—strip method

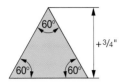

1. Square up the fabric (see page 72 for instructions).

2. Cut the fabric in strips as wide as the desired finished height of the triangle, plus ¾" for seam allowances. For example, to make a finished equilateral triangle that is 3" high, cut a 3¾"-wide fabric strip.

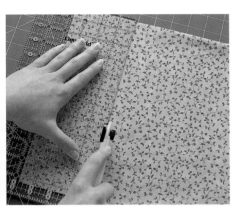

3. Align a ruler's 60° line with the long, lower edge of the strip and cut.

4. Rotate the ruler so the opposing 60° line is aligned with the same long, lower edge of the strip and cut.

5. Repeat steps 3 and 4 to work your way across the fabric strip and cut additional equilateral triangles.

QUICK REFERENCE CHART
YARDAGE ESTIMATOR: 60° EQUILATERAL TRIANGLES FROM STRIPS

Use this chart to determine the number of 60° equilateral triangles that can be cut from various yardages.

Cut fabric strips as wide as the desired height of the finished triangle, plus ¾".

Yardage figures include ¼" seam allowances and are based on 42"-long strips.

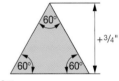

HEIGHT OF TRIANGLE		YARDAGE (44/45"-wide fabric)							
Finished	Cut Strip Width	¼	½	¾	1	1¼	1½	1¾	2
1"	1¾"	180	360	540	720	900	1,080	1,296	1,476
1½"	2¼"	120	240	360	480	600	720	840	960
2"	2¾"	66	132	198	286	352	418	484	572
2½"	3¼"	36	90	144	198	234	288	342	396
3"	3¾"	32	64	112	144	192	224	256	304
3½"	4¼"	28	56	84	112	140	168	196	224
4"	4¾"	12	36	60	84	108	132	156	180

tip When cutting an equilateral triangle, note that the ruler sometimes covers the shape you are cutting. It's easier and more efficient to move the ruler from one side of the shape to the other than to move the fabric strip or rotate the cutting mat.

QUICK TIP

Bending at the hip rather than at the waist when rotary-cutting is easier and puts less stress on your back and arms. To facilitate this, place your cutting mat on an appropriate height table or countertop.

QUICK REFERENCE CHART

SETTING TRIANGLES AND SETTING SQUARES

Use this chart to determine the correct size to cut side and corner setting triangles and setting squares based on the size of your finished block.

Finished Block Size	Size to cut square for side setting triangles *Formula A 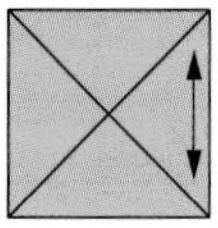	Size to cut square for corner setting triangles *Formula B 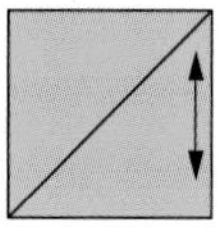	Size to cut setting squares *Formula C 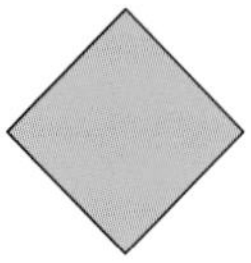
1"	2¾"	1⅝"	1½"
2"	4⅛"	2⅜"	2½"
3"	5½"	3"	3½"
4"	7"	3¾"	4½"
5"	8⅜"	4½"	5½"
6"	9¾"	5⅛"	6½"
7"	11¼"	5⅞"	7½"
8"	12⅝"	6⅝"	8½"
9"	14"	7¼"	9½"
10"	15½"	8"	10½"
11"	16⅞"	8¾"	11½"
12"	18¼"	9⅜"	12½"
13"	19¾"	10⅛"	13½"
14"	21⅛"	10⅞"	14½"
15"	22½"	11½"	15½"
16"	23⅞"	12¼"	16½"
17"	25⅜"	13"	17½"
18"	26¾"	13⅝"	18½"
19"	28⅛"	14⅜"	19½"
20"	29⅝"	15⅛"	20½"

- A—To calculate the size to cut a square for side setting triangles, multiply the finished block size by 1.414 and add 1.25" for seam allowances. (For example, 10" block ×1.414 = 14.14 + 1.25" = 15.39"; rounded up the measurement would be 15½".)

- B—To calculate the size to cut a square for corner setting triangles, divide the finished block size by 1.414 and add .875" for seam allowances. (For example, 10" block divided by 1.414 = 7.07 + .875" = 7.945"; rounded up the measurement would be 8".)

- C—To calculate the size to cut a setting square, add ½" to the finished block size to allow for seam allowances. (For example, 10" block + ½" = 10½".)

cutting setting triangles and blocks

Quilt blocks set on the diagonal (or "on point") may require setting triangles to fill out the design. These setting triangles are often called filler triangles. When quilt blocks are turned on the diagonal, it often means that the straight grain of the block is on the diagonal also.

To stabilize the fabric and control its natural tendency to sag, it is critical that the setting triangles are cut so that the straight grain runs up and down.

Some quilters prefer to cut triangles ½ to 1" larger than required and trim away the excess fabric after piecing the top. The measurements given in the chart opposite are mathematically correct and do not allow for any excess fabric. *Note:* To "float" the blocks in a diagonal set, cut the side and corner setting triangles up to 2" larger than the diagonal measurement of the block.

side triangles

Side setting triangles are quarter-square triangles; one square produces four side triangles.

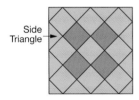

Side Triangle

To calculate the size to cut a square for setting triangles, multiply the finished block size by 1.414 and add 1¼" for seam allowances. (For example, 10" block × 1.414 = 14.14 + 1.25" = 15.39"; rounded up the measurement would be 15½".) Side triangle measurements for several standard block sizes are shown in the chart opposite.

corner triangles

Corner triangles are half-square triangles; one square yields two corner triangles.

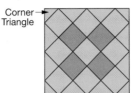

Corner Triangle

To calculate the size to cut a square for corner setting triangles, divide the finished block size by 1.414 and add .875" for seam allowances. (For example, 10" block divided by 1.414 = 7.07 + .875" = 7.945"; rounded up the measurement would be 8".) Shown opposite are corner triangle measurements for several standard block sizes.

setting squares

Setting squares are generally solid squares cut to place between pieced or appliquéd blocks to set off a design.

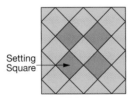

Setting Square

To calculate the size to cut a square for setting squares, add ½" to the finished block size to allow for seam allowances. (For example, 10" block + ½" = 10½".) Shown opposite are setting square measurements for several standard block sizes.

caring for your rotary cutter

- Always store your rotary cutter with the blade closed. Keep it out of the reach of children. Be certain to cut on a clean cutting mat; pins and other hard objects will make nicks in the blade.

- Periodically remove the blade from the cutter and carefully wipe away any lint and residue. Take the cutter apart, one piece at a time, laying out the parts in order. Add one drop of sewing machine oil around the center of the blade before reassembling the cutter.

- Replace blades as needed. Take the cutter apart one piece at a time, laying out the parts in order. Reassemble with a new blade. Dispose of the old blade using the new blade's packaging.

- High humidity can cause the rotary cutter blade to rust. To prevent this, store your rotary cutter in a cool, dry place.

QUICK TIP

Templates must be accurate or the error, no matter how small, will compound itself many times as the quilt is assembled.

marking with templates

A template is a thin, firm pattern that aids quilters as they cut the various fabric pieces needed for patchwork and appliqué work. The centuries-old process of cutting patchwork or appliqué pieces employs scissors and templates. Using a template may still be the best way to mark and cut curved or irregular-shape pieces, and many quilters use templates for traditional shapes, too. Commercially available acrylic templates are helpful for quick rotary cutting of specialty shapes and patterns, especially those that need to be cut in large multiples.

This section addresses templates made for both hand and machine piecing. Templates can be made from different materials. What you choose depends on how often they will be used. Make sure that your choice of template material will hold up to the wear that it receives from multiple tracings without wearing away at the edges.

Sturdy, durable material such as template plastic, available at quilt and crafts supply stores, is suitable for making your own permanent templates for scissors-cut pieces.

using templates for rotary cutting

Premade templates of thick plastic or acrylic material are often available at quilt shops in a variety of commonly used shapes. These templates are durable enough to be used with a rotary cutter, which speeds the cutting process.

1. Place the template faceup on the right side of an appropriately sized fabric strip.

2. Cut precisely around edges of template with a rotary cutter.

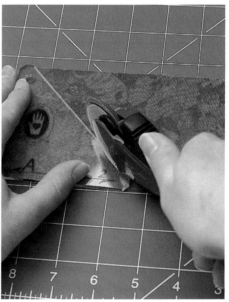

other template types

printed paper patterns

To eliminate the tracing step, sandwich a printed paper pattern between two pieces of template plastic, or one piece of template plastic and tag board or sandpaper. Use rubber cement or a glue stick to adhere the template plastic to the top of the pattern piece and the template plastic, tag board, or sandpaper to the back of the pattern piece. Let the adhesive dry before cutting through all layers at once to make an accurate template.

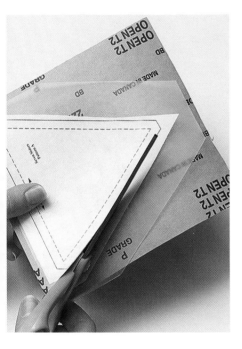

tip If your ruler is slipping when you put pressure on it, adhere small sandpaper dots to the underside of the ruler. They're available at quilt shops or you can make your own with a hole punch and fine-grain sandpaper.

flexible, see-through plastic sheeting

Available at quilt shops, this special-purpose, colored plastic uses static electricity to stick to the rotary-cutting ruler. It is used for do-it-yourself rotary-cutting template making. Cut the plastic to size and place on the rotary-cutting ruler as an aid in speedy cutting.

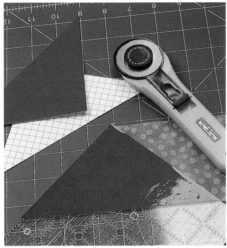

graph paper templates

You can use the printed lines on graph paper to draw a pattern piece. Glue the graph-paper pattern to template plastic, tag board, or cardboard. Allow the adhesive to dry before cutting through all layers at once to make an accurate template.

rotary-cutter troubleshooting

Is your cutter not cutting through all the layers? Check the following:

- Is the blade dull? If so, replace it and carefully dispose of the used one. Some blades may be successfully sharpened with a special tool.

- Is there a nick in the blade? You'll know if you discover evenly spaced uncut threads, the result of a blade section not touching the fabric during each rotation. Replace the blade. In the future, avoid cutting over pins and/or dropping the rotary cutter.

- Did you use enough pressure? If you don't have a dull blade but still find large areas where fabric layers weren't cut through cleanly, or where only the uppermost layers were cut, you may not be putting enough muscle behind the cutter. If the problem persists, try cutting fewer fabric layers at a time.

- Is your mat worn out? With extended use, grooves can be worn into your cutting mat, leaving the blade with not enough resistance to make clear cuts through the fabric.

tips for cutting borders

- Always cut on the straight grain of the fabric, never on the bias, because the bias has give and borders with give will cause the quilt to stretch out of shape over time.

- Cut the borders on the lengthwise grain (parallel to the selvage) if you have enough fabric. If cut from a single piece of fabric they will not need to be seamed and will rarely stretch.

- If you must cut the borders on the crosswise grain (perpendicular to the selvage) and seam them, sew them together with diagonal seams, which will be less visible. Borders cut on the crosswise grain have a bit more give and stretch than those cut on the lengthwise grain, and may stretch or sag over time.

QUICK REFERENCE CHART
DIAGONAL MEASUREMENTS OF SQUARES

Use this chart to determine quilt center size of a diagonally set quilt. For example, if blocks finish 12" and are set on point, quilt center size = (17" × number of blocks horizontally) + (17" × number of blocks vertically).

To calculate the finished diagonal measurement of a block, multiply finished block measurement (without seam allowances) by 1.414.

Shown below are diagonal measurements for several standard block sizes. Figures are rounded up to the nearest ⅛" (.125").

Finished Block Size	Finished Diagonal Measurement	Decimal Equivalent of Diagonal Measurement
1"	1½"	1.5"
1½"	2⅛"	2.125"
2"	2⅞"	2.875"
2½"	3⅝"	3.625"
3"	4¼"	4.25"
3½"	5"	5.0"
4"	5⅝"	5.625"
4½"	6⅜"	6.375"
5"	7⅛"	7.125"
5½"	7⅞"	7.875"
6"	8½"	8.5"
6½"	9¼"	9.25"
7"	10"	10.0"
7½"	10⅝"	10.625"
8"	11⅜"	11.375"
8½"	12⅛"	12.125"
9"	12¾"	12.75"
9½"	13½"	13.5"
10"	14¼"	14.25"
10½"	14⅞"	14.875"
11"	15⅝"	15.625"
11½"	16⅜"	16.375"
12"	17"	17.0"
12½"	17¾"	17.75"
13"	18½"	18.5"
14"	19⅞"	19.875"
15"	21¼"	21.25"
16"	22⅝"	22.625"
17"	24⅛"	24.125"
18"	25½"	25.5"
19"	26⅞"	26.875"
20"	28⅜"	28.375"

QUICK REFERENCE CHART
MAGIC NUMBERS FOR ROTARY CUTTING

To determine the cutting size of a variety of shapes when rotary-cutting, use this chart.

All measurements assume a ¼" seam allowance is being used.

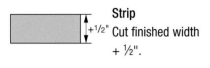

Strip
Cut finished width + ½".

Square and Rectangle
Cut finished size + ½".

Half-Square Triangle
Cut finished width + ⅞".

Quarter-Square Triangle
Cut finished width + 1¼".

Equilateral Triangle
Cut finished height + ¾".

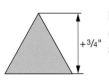

Isosceles Triangle-in-a-Square Center Triangle
Cut finished width + ⅞".

Isosceles Triangle-in-a-Square Side Triangle
Cut finished width + ¾", finished height + 1¼" (must be made in mirror images).

45° Diamond
Cut finished height + ½", finished width + ½".

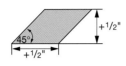

30° Diamond
Cut finished height + ½", finished width + ½".

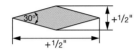

60° Diamond
Cut finished height + ½", finished width + ½".

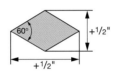

Hexagon
From a 60° diamond, cut finished height + ½", finished width + ½".

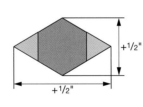

Octagon
From a square, cut finished height + ½", finished width + ½".

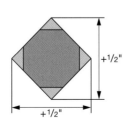

QUICK REFERENCE CHART
RULER AND CALCULATOR EQUIVALENTS

If you're trying to convert a calculated yardage or measurement into the nearest ruler equivalent, use this at-a-glance reference chart.

Ruler Fraction	Calculator Decimal
1/64	.016
1/32	.031
1/16	.0625
1/8	.125
3/16	.1875
1/4	.25
5/16	.3125
3/8	.375
7/16	.4375
1/2	.50
9/16	.5625
5/8	.625
11/16	.6875
3/4	.75
13/16	.8125
7/8	.875
15/16	.9375

QUICK REFERENCE CHART
YARDAGE AND METRIC EQUIVALENTS

If you need to convert a pattern's units of measurement, use this chart to determine the quantities needed.
Equivalents are for inches, yardage in eighths and decimals, and meters.

INCHES	YARDS (fractions)	YARDS (decimals)	METERS	INCHES	YARDS (fractions)	YARDS (decimals)	METERS
4½"	⅛ yd.	.125 yd.	.144 m	157½"	4⅜ yd.	4.375 yd.	4.001 m
9"	¼ yd.	.25 yd.	.229 m	162"	4½ yd.	4.5 yd.	4.115 m
12"	⅓ yd.	.333 yd.	.304 m	166½"	4⅝ yd.	4.625 yd.	4.229 m
13½"	⅜ yd.	.375 yd.	.343 m	171"	4¾ yd.	4.75 yd.	4.343 m
18"	½ yd.	.5 yd.	.457 m	180"	5 yd.	5.0 yd.	4.572 m
22½"	⅝ yd.	.625 yd.	.572 m	184½"	5⅛ yd.	5.125 yd.	4.686 m
24"	⅔ yd.	.667 yd.	.610 m	189"	5¼ yd.	5.25 yd.	4.801 m
27"	¾ yd.	.75 yd.	.686 m	193½"	5⅜ yd.	5.375 yd.	4.915 m
31½"	⅞ yd.	.875 yd.	.8 m	198"	5½ yd.	5.5 yd.	5.029 m
36"	1 yd.	1.0 yd.	.914 m	202½"	5⅝ yd.	5.625 yd.	5.144 m
40½"	1⅛ yd.	1.125 yd.	1.029 m	207"	5¾ yd.	5.75 yd.	5.258 m
45"	1¼ yd.	1.25 yd.	1.143 m	216"	6 yd.	6.0 yd.	5.486 m
48"	1⅓ yd.	1.333 yd.	1.219 m	220½"	6⅛ yd.	6.125 yd.	5.601 m
49½"	1⅜ yd.	1.375 yd.	1.257 m	225"	6¼ yd.	6.25 yd.	5.715 m
54"	1½ yd.	1.5 yd.	1.372 m	229½"	6⅜ yd.	6.375 yd.	5.829 m
58½"	1⅝ yd.	1.625 yd.	1.486 m	234"	6½ yd.	6.5 yd.	5.944 m
60"	1⅔ yd.	1.667 yd.	1.524 m	238½"	6⅝ yd.	6.625 yd.	6.058 m
63"	1¾ yd.	1.75 yd.	1.6 m	243"	6¾ yd.	6.75 yd.	6.172 m
67½"	1⅞ yd.	1.875 yd.	1.715 m	252"	7 yd.	7.0 yd.	6.401 m
72"	2 yd.	2.0 yd.	1.829 m	256½"	7⅛ yd.	7.125 yd.	6.515 m
76½"	2⅛ yd.	2.125 yd.	1.943 m	261"	7¼ yd.	7.25 yd.	6.629 m
81"	2¼ yd.	2.25 yd.	2.057 m	265½"	7⅜ yd.	7.375 yd.	6.744 m
84"	2⅓ yd.	2.333 yd.	2.134 m	270"	7½ yd.	7.5 yd.	6.858 m
85½"	2⅜ yd.	2.375 yd.	2.172 m	274½"	7⅝ yd.	7.625 yd.	6.972 m
90"	2½ yd.	2.5 yd.	2.286 m	279"	7¾ yd.	7.75 yd.	7.087 m
94½"	2⅝ yd.	2.625 yd.	2.4 m	288"	8 yd.	8.0 yd.	7.315 m
96"	2⅔ yd.	2.667 yd.	2.438 m	292½"	8⅛ yd.	8.125 yd.	7.43 m
99"	2¾ yd.	2.75 yd.	2.515 m	297"	8¼ yd.	8.25 yd.	7.544 m
108"	3 yd.	3.0 yd.	2.743 m	301½"	8⅜ yd.	8.375 yd.	7.658 m
112½"	3⅛ yd.	3.125 yd.	2.858 m	306"	8½ yd.	8.5 yd.	7.772 m
117"	3¼ yd.	3.25 yd.	2.972 m	310½"	8⅝ yd.	8.625 yd.	7.887 m
120"	3⅓ yd.	3.333 yd.	3.048 m	315"	8¾ yd.	8.75 yd.	8.001 m
121½"	3⅜ yd.	3.375 yd.	3.086 m	324"	9 yd.	9.0 yd.	8.23 m
126"	3½ yd.	3.5 yd.	3.2 m	328½"	9⅛ yd.	9.125 yd.	8.344 m
130½"	3⅝ yd.	3.625 yd.	3.315 m	333"	9¼ yd.	9.25 yd.	8.458 m
132"	3⅔ yd.	3.667 yd.	3.353 m	337½"	9⅜ yd.	9.375 yd.	8.573 m
135"	3¾ yd.	3.75 yd.	3.429 m	342"	9½ yd.	9.5 yd.	8.687 m
144"	4 yd.	4.0 yd.	3.658 m	346½"	9⅝ yd.	9.625 yd.	8.801 m
148½"	4⅛ yd.	4.125 yd.	3.772 m	351"	9¾ yd.	9.75 yd.	8.915 m
153"	4¼ yd.	4.25 yd.	3.886 m	360"	10 yd.	10.0 yd.	9.144 m

QUICK REFERENCE CHART
YARDAGE WIDTH CONVERSION

If the width of your fabric is different than what the pattern calls for, use this chart to determine the yardage needed.

Yardage conversions are from 44/45"-wide fabric to 36"- or 58/60"-wide fabrics.

44/45"-wide	36"-wide	58/60"-wide	44/45"-wide	36"-wide	58/60"-wide
1/8 yd.	1/4 yd.	1/8 yd.	4 3/8 yd.	5 1/2 yd.	3 1/3 yd.
1/4 yd.	1/3 yd.	1/4 yd.	4 1/2 yd.	5 5/8 yd.	3 1/2 yd.
1/3 yd.	1/2 yd.	1/3 yd.	4 5/8 yd.	5 7/8 yd.	3 5/8 yd.
3/8 yd.	1/2 yd.	1/3 yd.	4 3/4 yd.	6 yd.	3 5/8 yd.
1/2 yd.	5/8 yd.	1/2 yd.	5 yd.	6 1/4 yd.	3 7/8 yd.
5/8 yd.	7/8 yd.	1/2 yd.	5 1/8 yd.	6 1/2 yd.	4 yd.
2/3 yd.	7/8 yd.	5/8 yd.	5 1/4 yd.	6 5/8 yd.	4 yd.
3/4 yd.	1 yd.	5/8 yd.	5 3/8 yd.	6 3/4 yd.	4 1/8 yd.
7/8 yd.	1 1/8 yd.	2/3 yd.	5 1/2 yd.	6 7/8 yd.	4 1/4 yd.
1 yd.	1 1/4 yd.	7/8 yd.	5 5/8 yd.	7 1/8 yd.	4 1/3 yd.
1 1/8 yd.	1 1/2 yd.	7/8 yd.	5 3/4 yd.	7 1/4 yd.	4 3/8 yd.
1 1/4 yd.	1 5/8 yd.	1 yd.	6 yd.	7 1/2 yd.	4 5/8 yd.
1 1/3 yd.	1 2/3 yd.	1 1/8 yd.	6 1/8 yd.	7 2/3 yd.	4 3/4 yd.
1 3/8 yd.	1 3/4 yd.	1 1/8 yd.	6 1/4 yd.	7 3/4 yd.	4 7/8 yd.
1 1/2 yd.	1 7/8 yd.	1 1/4 yd.	6 3/8 yd.	8 yd.	4 7/8 yd.
1 5/8 yd.	2 1/8 yd.	1 1/4 yd.	6 1/2 yd.	8 1/8 yd.	5 yd.
1 2/3 yd.	2 1/8 yd.	1 1/3 yd.	6 5/8 yd.	8 1/3 yd.	5 1/8 yd.
1 3/4 yd.	2 1/4 yd.	1 1/3 yd.	6 3/4 yd.	8 1/2 yd.	5 1/8 yd.
1 7/8 yd.	2 3/8 yd.	1 1/2 yd.	7 yd.	8 3/4 yd.	5 1/3 yd.
2 yd.	2 1/2 yd.	1 5/8 yd.	7 1/8 yd.	9 yd.	5 1/2 yd.
2 1/8 yd.	2 2/3 yd.	1 5/8 yd.	7 1/4 yd.	9 1/8 yd.	5 1/2 yd.
2 1/4 yd.	2 7/8 yd.	1 3/4 yd.	7 3/8 yd.	9 1/4 yd.	5 5/8 yd.
2 1/3 yd.	3 yd.	1 7/8 yd.	7 1/2 yd.	9 3/8 yd.	5 3/4 yd.
2 3/8 yd.	3 yd.	1 7/8 yd.	7 5/8 yd.	9 5/8 yd.	5 7/8 yd.
2 1/2 yd.	3 1/8 yd.	2 yd.	7 3/4 yd.	9 3/4 yd.	6 yd.
2 5/8 yd.	3 1/4 yd.	2 yd.	8 yd.	10 yd.	6 1/8 yd.
2 2/3 yd.	3 1/3 yd.	2 1/8 yd.	8 1/8 yd.	10 1/4 yd.	6 1/4 yd.
2 3/4 yd.	3 1/2 yd.	2 1/8 yd.	8 1/4 yd.	10 1/3 yd.	6 1/3 yd.
2 7/8 yd.	3 5/8 yd.	2 1/4 yd.	8 3/8 yd.	10 1/2 yd.	6 3/8 yd.
3 yd.	3 3/4 yd.	2 1/3 yd.	8 1/2 yd.	10 5/8 yd.	6 1/2 yd.
3 1/8 yd.	4 yd.	2 3/8 yd.	8 5/8 yd.	10 7/8 yd.	6 5/8 yd.
3 1/4 yd.	4 1/8 yd.	2 1/2 yd.	8 3/4 yd.	11 yd.	6 3/4 yd.
3 3/8 yd.	4 1/4 yd.	2 5/8 yd.	9 yd.	11 1/4 yd.	6 7/8 yd.
3 1/2 yd.	4 3/8 yd.	2 2/3 yd.	9 1/8 yd.	11 1/2 yd.	7 yd.
3 5/8 yd.	4 5/8 yd.	2 3/4 yd.	9 1/4 yd.	11 5/8 yd.	7 1/8 yd.
3 3/4 yd.	4 3/4 yd.	2 7/8 yd.	9 3/8 yd.	11 3/4 yd.	7 1/8 yd.
3 7/8 yd.	4 7/8 yd.	3 yd.	9 1/2 yd.	11 7/8 yd.	7 1/4 yd.
4 yd.	5 yd.	3 1/8 yd.	9 5/8 yd.	12 yd.	7 1/3 yd.
4 1/8 yd.	5 1/4 yd.	3 1/4 yd.	9 3/4 yd.	12 1/4 yd.	7 1/2 yd.
4 1/4 yd.	5 1/3 yd.	3 1/4 yd.	10 yd.	12 1/2 yd.	7 5/8 yd.

quilting basics

Read through these general quilting instructions to ensure you'll properly cut and assemble your quilt. Accuracy in each step guarantees a successful quiltmaking experience.

basic tools

Acrylic ruler: To aid in making perfectly straight cuts with a rotary cutter, choose a ruler of thick, clear plastic. Many sizes are available. A 6×24" ruler marked in ¼" increments with 30°, 45°, and 60° angles is a good first purchase.

Rotary-cutting mat: A rotary cutter should always be used with a mat designed specifically for it. In addition to protecting the table, the mat helps keep the fabric from shifting while you cut. Often these mats are described as self-healing, meaning the blade does not leave slash marks or grooves in the surface, even after repeated usage.

Rotary cutter: The round blade of a rotary cutter will cut up to six layers of fabric at once. Because the blade is so sharp, be sure to purchase one with a safety guard and keep the guard over the blade when you're not cutting. The blade can be removed from the handle and replaced when it gets dull.

Scissors: You'll need one pair for cutting fabric and another for cutting paper and plastic.

Pencils and other marking tools: Marks made with special quilt markers are easy to remove after sewing.

Template plastic: This slightly frosted plastic comes in sheets about 1/16" thick.

Iron and ironing board: Pressing the seams ensures accurate piecing.

Sewing thread: Use 100% cotton thread.

Sewing machine: Any machine in good working order with well-adjusted tension will produce pucker-free patchwork seams.

choose your fabrics

Most quilters prefer 100% cotton fabrics for quiltmaking. Cotton fabric minimizes seam distortion, presses crisply, and is easy to quilt. Most patterns, including those in this book, specify quantities for 44/45"-wide fabrics unless otherwise noted. Our projects call for a little extra yardage in length to allow for minor errors and slight shrinkage.

prepare your fabrics

Prewashing fabric offers quilters certainty as its main advantage. Today's fabrics resist bleeding and shrinkage, but some of both can occur in certain fabrics. Some quilters find prewashed fabric easier to quilt. If you choose to prewash your fabric, press it well before cutting.

Other quilters prefer the crispness of unwashed fabric, especially for machine piecing. And, if you use fabrics with the same fiber content throughout a quilt, then any shrinkage that occurs in its first washing should be uniform. Some quilters find this small amount of shrinkage desirable, because it gives a quilt a slightly puckered, antique look.

We recommend you prewash a scrap of each fabric to test it for shrinkage and bleeding. If you choose to prewash an entire fabric piece, unfold it to a single layer. Wash it in warm water to allow the fabric to shrink and/or bleed. If the fabric bleeds, rinse it until the water runs clear. Do not use it in a quilt if it hasn't stopped bleeding. Hang the fabric to dry, or tumble it in the dryer until slightly damp; press well.

trace templates

To mark on fabric, use a pencil, white dressmaker's pencil, chalk, or a special fabric marker that makes a thin, accurate line. Do not use a ballpoint or ink pen; it may bleed if washed. Test all marking tools on a fabric scrap before using them.

Templates used to make pieces for machine piecing have seam allowances included so you can use common lines for efficient cutting. Place a template facedown on the wrong side of the fabric and trace; repeat, but do not leave spaces between the tracings. Using a rotary cutter and ruler, cut precisely on the drawn (cutting) lines.

mitering borders

To add a border with mitered corners, first pin a border strip to a quilt top edge, matching the center of the strip and the center of the quilt top edge. Sew together, beginning and ending the seam ¼" from the quilt top corners (see Diagram 1, *opposite top*). Allow excess border fabric to extend beyond the edges. Repeat with remaining border strips. Press the seam allowances toward the border strips.

At one corner, lap one border strip over the other (see Diagram 2, *opposite top*). Align

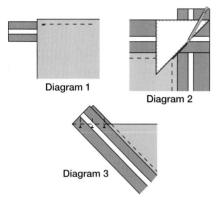

Diagram 1

Diagram 2

Diagram 3

the edge of a 90° right triangle with the raw edge of the top strip so the long edge of the triangle intersects the border seam in the corner. With a pencil, draw along the edge of the triangle from the seam out to the raw edge. Place the bottom border strip on top and repeat the marking process.

With the right sides together, match the marked seam lines and pin (see Diagram 3).

Beginning with a backstitch at the inside corner, sew together the strips, stitching exactly on the marked lines. Check the right side to see that the corner lies flat. Trim the excess fabric, leaving a ¼" seam allowance. Press the seam open. Mark and sew the remaining corners in the same manner.

finishing

LAYERING

Cut and piece the backing fabric to measure at least 3" longer on all sides than the quilt top. Press all seam allowances open. With wrong sides together, layer the quilt top and backing fabric with the batting in between; baste. Quilt as desired.

BINDING

The binding for most quilts is cut on the straight grain of the fabric. If your quilt has curved edges, cut the strips on the bias. The cutting instructions for projects in this book specify the number of binding strips or a total length needed to finish the quilt. The instructions also specify enough width for a French-fold, or double-layer, binding because it's easier to apply and adds durability.

Join the strips with diagonal seams to make one continuous binding strip (see Diagram 4, *below*). Trim the excess fabric, leaving ¼" seam allowances. Press seam allowances open. Then, with the wrong sides together, fold under 1" at one end of the binding strip (see Diagram 5, *below*); press. Fold the strip in half lengthwise (see Diagram 6, *below*); press.

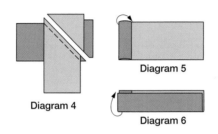

Diagram 4

Diagram 5

Diagram 6

Beginning in the center of one side, place the binding strip against the right side of the quilt top, aligning the binding strip's raw edges with the quilt top's raw edge (see Diagram 7, *right*). Beginning 1½" from the folded edge, sew through all layers, stopping ¼" from the corner. Backstitch, then clip the threads. Remove the quilt from under the sewing-machine presser foot.

Fold the binding strip upward (see Diagram 8, *right*), creating a diagonal fold, and finger-press.

Holding the diagonal fold in place with your finger, bring the binding strip down in line with the next edge, making a horizontal fold that aligns with the first edge of the quilt (see Diagram 9, *right*).

Start sewing again at the top of the horizontal fold, stitching through all layers. Sew around the quilt, turning each corner in the same manner.

When you return to the starting point, lap the binding strip inside the beginning fold (see Diagram 10, *right*). Finish sewing to the starting point (see Diagram 11, *right*). Trim the batting and backing fabric even with the quilt top edges.

Turn the binding over the edge of the quilt to the back. Hand-stitch the

binding to the backing fabric, making sure to cover any machine stitching.

To make mitered corners on the back, hand-stitch the binding up to a corner; fold a miter in the binding. Take a stitch or two in the fold to secure it. Then stitch the binding in place up to the next corner. Finish each corner in the same manner.

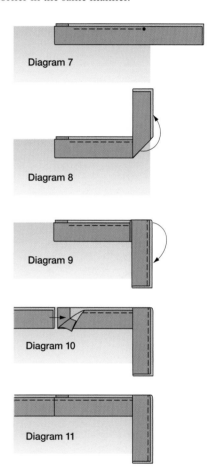

Diagram 7

Diagram 8

Diagram 9

Diagram 10

Diagram 11

Better Homes and Gardens®
Creative Collection™

Editorial Director
Gayle Goodson Butler

Executive Editor Karman Wittry Hotchkiss

Contributing Editorial Manager Heidi Palkovic

Contributing Design Director Tracy DeVenney

Contributing Graphic Designer Wendy Musgrave
Copy Chief Mary Heaton
Contributing Copy Editor Angela Ingle
Contributing Proofreaders Joleen Ross
Mary Helen Schiltz
Administrative Assistant Lori Eggers

Executive Vice President
Bob Mate

Publishing Group President
Jack Griffin

Chairman and CEO William T. Kerr
President and COO Stephen M. Lacy

In Memoriam
E. T. Meredith III (1933–2003)